sportin' ladies

herb michelson

sportin' ladies... confessions of the bimbos

chilton book company
radnor, pennsylvania

Copyright © 1975 by Herbert A. Michelson
First Edition   All Rights Reserved

Published in Radnor, Pa., by Chilton Book Company
and simultaneously in Ontario, Canada
by Thomas Nelson & Sons, Ltd.
Designed by Adrianne Onderdonk Dudden
Manufactured in the United States of America

Library of Congress Cataloging in Publication Data

Michelson, Herb.
   Sportin' ladies . . . : confessions of the bimbos.

   1. Prostitution—United States.   I. Title.
HQ144.M53   301.41'74'444   74-20595
ISBN 0-8019-5942-X

contents

This belongs to the Bimbos, here and elsewhere

introduction

The Bimbos. The girls who do, or would like to do. Women who fancy jocks but are otherwise unprogrammed. Annies, Shirleys, Groupies, Starfuckers; that's what the men call them. Yes, and no. There must have been an Annie once someplace, and there are Shirleys now seemingly every place. But not Groupies, for that's generational. And really not Starfuckers, because they will have sex with "civilians," too. Just keep it at the Bimbo level, where it is manageable and understandable and realistic. Don't make too much of her, but don't demean her. She is not seeking beatification, but don't burn her at the stake either. Let her have her fun, her enjoyment, her excitement, her flurry of ego satisfaction, her spasm of sexual pleasure. Somewhere along the line, some jock will give her a good time. That's all she wants. More would be nice, she knows. But she also knows that when you're a Bimbo, you have to settle for less. There is often sadness in her fun, price-paying moments of self-search, self-guilt, fear of the loneliness that might be waiting when there are no more other ball games to play. A Bimbo doesn't kid herself forever because she knows the ground rules; life will probably screw her just like all those other guys did. But she knows, too, that screwing can work two ways. Believe me; rather, believe the Bimbos.

0

You want a frame of reference? All right, here are three: the woman who shot Eddie Waitkus; the woman being held upside down in a shower by a professional football player; the woman in Cesar Cedeno's motel room.

vii

A fantasizing Bimbo, a working Bimbo, an incomplete Bimbo. One ruled insane, one tuned up, one dead.

And now to freeze the frames...

1. Ruth Ann Steinhagen had first seen Eddie Waitkus some twenty-six months before the night she shot him in the chest. The day of the first sighting, April 27, 1947, Waitkus was playing first base for the Chicago Cubs. The evening of the shooting, June 14, 1949, he was again in Chicago, only now as a player with the Philadelphia Phillies. Between those two dates, Miss Steinhagen developed a remarkably unfulfilled infatuation for the blond bachelor ballplayer: his number was 36, so she collected phonograph records produced in the year 1936; he was of Lithuanian extraction, so she studied the language; he was from Boston, so she ate baked beans habitually. Her room was a shrine of Eddie Waitkus photographs and newspapers clippings. She persistently fantasized his presence: they walked together, talked together, but they never had any physical relationship, in either fact or fantasy. There is no reason to believe that Ruth Ann ever spoke to Eddie Waitkus or came within an arm's length of him until the night she shot him. No reason at all. She wouldn't have dared.

"My first idea," Ruth Ann told a court attaché who was investigating her behavioral patterns, "was that I would shoot him because I liked him a great deal and knew I never could have him. And if I couldn't have him, neither could anybody else." She said she dreamed about killing him. Six weeks before the shooting, Miss Steinhagen and a close girlfriend went to a pawnshop to buy a gun. The twenty-two caliber rifle cost Ruth Ann twenty-one dollars. She learned how to assemble and disassemble the weapon and how to load it, then she checked the Chicago Cub schedule and reserved a room at the Edgewater Beach Hotel on the dates the Phillies were next due in town.

On the afternoon of June 14, the five-foot ten-inch tall, nineteen-year-old Miss Steinhagen attended the Cub–Philly game in Wrigley Field. Ruth Ann left the game early and alone and went to her room at the Edgewater Beach. The gun was already there. She left a note for Waitkus saying she would like to meet him and was asleep when he telephoned late that evening. She asked that he come to her room, and in about thirty minutes the twenty-nine-year-old first baseman knocked on her door.

Miss Steinhagen told the felony court's investigator that she "was scared stiff. But I thought to myself that I will settle this once and for all and really kill him. At that time, I had a knife in my shirt pocket and was going to use that on him. When I opened the door, he came rushing in right past me...I was kind of mad that he came right in and sat down and didn't give me a chance to stab him." She said she told Waitkus she had "a surprise" for him, then went to the closet, grabbed the gun, pointed it at him, told him to stand up and move over toward a window. Ruth Ann said that while she spoke, Eddie Waitkus "had a silly look on his face."

While Waitkus was asking Ruth Ann what this was all about, she shot him in the right chest, the bullet puncturing his lung and lodging not far from his heart. She remembered saying, "For two years, you have been bothering me, and now you are going to die...", and then pulling the trigger.

After Waitkus had fallen, Ruth Ann said she clasped his hand, briefly.

She was seated in an anteroom of the Chicago court when Waitkus was wheeled along to the trial. Someone asked her if she was thrilled to see him. "And how," said Ruth Ann. "I always will be." She was adjudged insane and committed to the state hospital at Kankakee, Illinois, for three years.

Waitkus was operated on twice, but recovered in time to play for the Phillies in their pennant-winning season of 1950. He led all National League first basemen in fielding that year, batted .284 and was named the majors' "Comeback Player of the Year." He was married in 1951, retired from baseball in 1955, died in Boston in 1972.

Not long after the shooting, while still recuperating in a hospital, Waitkus and a reporter spoke about Ruth Ann

Steinhagen's motives and infatuation. Eddie Waitkus said, "Why did that silly honey do that?"

2. The name of the National Football League team is not important. Neither is the name of the town the club was visiting, nor the identity of the woman. Forget what hotel it was, too.

The way the story's told—and it is too real to have been invented—nearly every player on the club had a go at this one lovely creature in this one room on this one night. Hour, after hour, after hour.

She went through the entire roster at least once. It's possible even members of the taxi squad got theirs. But the evening was still young. A large lineman (there has never been a small lineman) grabbed the lady, dragged her into the shower, held her upside down directly under the spigot for many minutes, then returned her to the huddled masses with these words: "All right you guys, I cleaned her out and she's ready to go again."

3. Altagracia De La Cruz was nineteen years old and had known Houston Astro outfielder Cesar Cedeno for at least one year at the time of her death. She was killed on December 10, 1973, in a motel room in Santo Domingo by Cedeno's thirty-eight caliber pistol. He said he tried to take the weapon from her, but that it fired. He was convicted of involuntary manslaughter and fined one hundred dollars. At the time, he was twenty-three years old and married. He was the second leading hitter in the National League in 1973, and said that the shooting would not affect his play in 1974. He said the tragedy "will help me be a better person." He also said that he would be ready for the start of spring training.

()

Bear in mind that Bimbo-ology isn't limited to professional athletes, that there are sportswriter Bimbos, politican

Bimbos, the much-publicized rock music world groupies, and...

In November of 1973, a nineteen-year-old Arkansas lass said she'd had sexual relations with nearly half of the eleven-hundred man police force of Memphis, Tennessee. A police official suggested her claim was exaggerated. Less than twenty officers were being investigated, he said.

And she said, "I like cops."

()

From the start, it is easy for the athlete to get laid. It is no trouble at all. It comes with the deal, is issued with the high school letter sweater. The athlete needn't reapply for sex as he would a passport or a driver's license; the lay is for the duration—career permanence. The men among the boys don't flaunt it. The availability is taken for granted, and if the wise ones need it, they know where to find it, discreetly. The others, the boys in men's bodies and uniforms, are less discreet. They also take it for granted, but unlike their mature teammates they take it where they can get it.

In high school, the athlete is identifiable, and sought. His romantic pattern is predictable: he will bundle with all the hot numbers while giving his letter sweater to the prettiest girl in the cafeteria. He needs both and always will. He wants to be seen publicly with a vision of wholesome loveliness. He wants to get his rocks off with whomever brings knowledge, flair, and enthusiasm to her work. He is young, after all, and willing to learn. He covets the All-American girl *and* an All-American lay, nominally unavailable in the same package. The Bimbo gets the picture. Not the ring, just the picture. She does not see herself as the wife and, in fact, will strive valiantly not to become an athlete's wife. Who, better than the Bimbo, is aware of all the Bimbos out there? Well, the wife is, but the wife, as you will learn through one (Mrs. Sal

Bando), cannot permit herself to think about these things. The Bimbos can empathize with the wives and truly wish them no harm, for it's quite apparent, and acceptable, to the Bimbos that there is yet a third ball game—home and kids and such—beyond the other ball game. Everything in its place, and a place for everything. The good Bimbos don't want to be threatened by security. It unnerves them, makes them want to move on, just as the wife doesn't wish to be threatened by insecurity and the possibility of discovering infidelities that will, by society's standards, force *her* to move on. Teamwork in action, and seated there in the stands, looking but not really seeing, is our friend the athlete. If all works well for him, he won't have to come to terms; he can be a holdout and still play. His vision has no limitations.

The sportswriter's functional euphemism is "personal problems." A professional athlete is not hitting line drives, or missing layups, or dropping passes in the seams of a zone. He is in a slump, and he is often in a slump because of "personal problems." You, the fan, the reader of the sports pages, accept the explanation. The sportswriter has trained you to stop right there, to treat your slumping hero with kindness because the poor sonofagun has "personal problems." Explain an error with compassion, not derision. And never, never, never ask: "What personal problems?" Never wonder if the player has knocked up a chick, been caught diddling by his old lady, or is laid low with a "groin injury" that travels in lesser circles under the identity of V.D. Perish such thoughts. They are dangerous.

What will our small children say were they to read that their favorite center fielder has the clap. "How," the child will ask the older fan in the house, "did my favorite center fielder get the clap, daddy? And tell me, daddy do, what is the clap?" The clap, son, is a "personal problem, a groin injury, an ailment that will keep our hero on the sidelines for a few days. That's all you have to know." The sportswriter has trained daddy well.

The Bimbo, with her Lamont Cranston-like power to cloud men's minds, knows. Indeed she knows. She does not have to read between the lines; she *is* between the lines. The prudent bookmaker can often get better information from a Bimbo than a columnist, for our girl's judgment penetrates beyond statistics. The Bimbo, God bless her, knows. And how. A girl who calls herself Maggie, and who is identified further along as "The Little Yellow Butterfly," points out with immense accuracy and simplicity that she can get to know an athlete in ways no sportswriter ever will. *Ever.* Don't give Maggie any of this "personal problems" bullshit. She knows how the game is played. The athletes only participate, but the Bimbos understand.

()

The premise for this book reared during one of those baseball park events they call "Camera Day." Ropes are strung down the base lines; the players stand between the ropes and their dugouts; fans with cameras troop onto the field and are given fifteen minutes to click and ogle.

"I get more phone numbers at a 'Camera Day' than anyplace else," a pitcher said quietly to an observer. "Just watch."

Sure enough, several of the young ladies who were taking pictures were also passing scraps of paper to the athletes they were photographing. If you weren't watching for it, you wouldn't have noticed. Wide receivers and Bimbos have the good hands.

Twenty minutes later, the pitcher pulled one hundred sunflower seeds and thirty-five phone numbers out of his back pocket.

"My God, you mean to tell me there are that many opportunities to make out?"

"One of your slower 'Camera Days'," said the pitcher.

()

Spend enough time in clubhouses and you hear them talk about the Bimbos. Most of the players do it with tee-hee bawdiness. They tend to demean the women who play with the pros.

Read enough sports biographies and you learn the athlete's attitude toward the Bimbos: pornographic and self-serving and giggly.

That's understandable among these guys. When you realize that many colleges have a flock of budding Bimbos waiting to greet potential athletic department recruits during weekend campus visits, you can contend with the cynicism of the jock. It's just his way.

But what about the Bimbo's way, her point of view, her right to tee-hee the jock? Where are her memoirs?

There is this lady in Missouri who for many, many years encountered many, many umpires and many, many college basketball coaches. She is in the same bar as an observer one night. They are introduced, they drink, she talks.

"I could fill a book," she says.

"Why don't you?" she's asked.

"Don't want my little girl to find out what her mother's been doing all these years," she says.

She will be given an alias, but there is no interest. And the evening ends. The evening, not the premise.

()

The Bimbos who would talk were guaranteed the following:

1. They could use whatever name they wished. None permitted use of her own.

2. Athletes with whom they diddled would be unidentified, unless the Bimbo wished otherwise. Only one, Tina, insisted

on using the player's name. Under no other condition would she grant the interview.

3. Places, team names, positions—on the field, not in bed—would be changed if the Bimbo so wished. Most so wished.

4. It was their story to tell as they wanted; editing would be done in terms of continuity and not viewpoint.

5. They would not be mocked or condemned.

Because of these guarantees, the reader must resist making wild identity guesses. Still, there's a good chance that by the time the reader runs the course of Bimbos, any guess might be accurate. I mean, we're dealing with big numbers here.

0

How, they ask, did I go about finding them? All I can tell you is that the Bimbos seemed to keep turning up, as did people who knew Bimbos or people who knew people who knew Bimbos. To be a Bimbo, the lady must be visible. I was hesitant to speak to too many athletes about the project for fear their attitudes would interfere with my basic concern for the ladies. Of course, I received the permission of Oakland A's third baseman Sal Bando to interview his wife, Sandy, and I did call on another player's rich store of personal lore on the famed Chicago Shirley when I assumed she was unavailable for comment.

Several months into the work, I had been unable to find a black Bimbo. Many black professional athletes date only white women, and I wanted a black woman's point of view on this subject. Two black baseball players promised to look around but never delivered. Finally, a black non-athlete set up introductions to the women I call Claudia and Sue Ann.

One former major league pitcher of little distinction was long rumored to be a treasure trove of Bimbo-ology. The word was that this much-traveled young man possessed the world's most erotically detailed little black book. The book, as legend had it, contained names, addresses, phone numbers, physical descriptions, and specialties. Yes, specialties, each coded. Take our friend Maggie and her strawberry jam fetish, for example. Were the pitcher to have encountered Maggie, he might assign to her number 863½, let's say. His book was supposedly rife with these coded tidbits that only he could understand. Had he spent as much time studying batters as Bimbos, he might still be in the majors. Yet, I'm not fully convinced of the truth of his conquests because not one of our Bimbos mentioned his name. So I never did seek him or his book, and as it turned out Bimbos are rarely fetishists anyway. As several of them told me, "There are only so many ways you can do it, and after a time you end up with the one or two that are comfortable and pretty standard." Maggie just happened to dig strawberry jam, and Sue Ann just happened to end up with guys who needed additional entertainment while making love. Pauline's dildo-bearing golf pro was a rarity, and sodomists seemed not to be in flower during my Bimbo season. The ladies do have their standards.

()

The girls who play the sports game do have a surface sameness about them, no question. Research indicated that there are enough Bimbo stewardesses in this land to start a new transcontinental airline. References to stews attending team parties cropped up in many non-stew interviews. Stewardesses simply have the opportunities: they lay over (sorry about that!) in towns where professional athletes may be laying over. And with so many pro clubs flying charters, the chemistry is bound to ignite. Stews play, too, but few of them with the freneticism of, let's say, our busy, busy lady Marianne.

The latter, whom I label, with no malice aforethought, "The Basic Bimbo," has covered so much ground in so many sports that I would hope industry might call on her as a prototype should mass production in this field become necessary. "All of 'em—ping-pong players, you name it," she says, with only a small measure of conceit. Obviously, all the adventures of a Marianne and several others aren't totally verifiable. One can't call an athlete and ask him if he balled so-and-so on such-and-such a date. To begin with, he well might have forgotten. To end with, he would want to know why I want to know. Yet, there are ways of checking, and I live under the assumption that at least ninety percent of what every Bimbo told me indeed took place. Because they were given the right to tell their stories their way, embellishment is excusable. But interestingly, the reverse was often more true: most of the ladies tended to duck questions about the extent of their involvements; the number of their affairs was at first minimized, although by the end of the taping sessions they often "remembered" incidents that had slipped their minds earlier. One example: Pauline, the married Bimbo, initially told me she'd bedded with a dozen professional golfers in her time. Later, she said, "Since I told you there were twelve, I've been thinking and trying to remember. I guess it was really more like twenty." Another example: Mildred, the grandmother Bimbo, shrugged off any mention of orgy incidents for the first few hours in our two sessions but eventually recalled servicing two groups, and I do mean groups, of pro football players on two separate occasions.

But we were talking about variety and the difficulty in obtaining enough "different" Bimbos. Several would tell me in our initial telephone conversations, when I would outline in very general terms the book's premise, that they felt I wouldn't be interested in their experiences. But it never hurt to talk about them. And in nearly every case in a public place, at first.

I didn't know any of the Bimbos before our meetings. A few I had heard about—usually from another Bimbo—but had never seen. Well, let me take that back. I had met our friend Gert of "The Gert and Gladys Show" years earlier in the Midwest, but only briefly. And not in any Bimbo context. Neither Gert, nor her friend Gladys, were approached in terms of plucking their personal sexual adventures. I wanted them because they, I reckoned, were long-time observers of the Bimbo scene and might prove excellent stage-setters. Gert has worked in the offices of several professional sports teams; Gladys was a desk clerk at a large hotel in which many teams stayed. These two women, as well as any psychologist, could, I felt, provide clues, so a trip to the Midwest seemed propitious. But as the interview progressed, and their wine-fueled nostalgia percolated, "The Gert and Gladys Show" followed a delightfully improvisational scenario, as you will see.

But other than Gert, all the Bimbo faces were new to me. In all cases, I used references on initial contact. And the references were mostly other Bimbos. Typically, one lady would conclude an interview by suggesting I chat with her friend so-and-so, and often she would phone the friend on the spot. These are gracious, helpful women, believe me.

There were some Bimbo leads, however, in which the sources did not wish to be revealed. For instance: "Here's Petunia's phone number, but don't tell her where you got it!" In those situations, I would tell the latest Bimbo I got her name "from a mutual friend." The gal's curiosity about the identity of said friend was often overwhelming. I'd let them guess, but I kept the faith. It's amusing to recall that one Bimbo to whom I was led by "a mutual friend" then directed me toward another, but with the instruction I was to say "a mutual friend sent me."

Only one of the Bimbos I turned up ducked a taping session. She claimed illness, but I didn't believe it and bothered her no more. And only one of those who did agree to be interviewed backed off from frankness in mid-interview. She seemed terribly frightened. I pressed for a time, but not with much vigor, because after all it was her deal and not mine. Yet she's here—the "fresh and innocent" one named

Kay; she's here because she's different, and reluctant. And her reluctance is rather fascinating, because the woman I call Pauline, the married Bimbo, bedded with the same professional golfer years earlier and spoke about it with little hesitation. Both women, however, are deeply fearful of repercussions, for unrelated reasons. They are a thousand miles and many years apart, but someday I would like to bring them together and then leave the room. They would have much to discuss. A married Bimbo willing to be interviewed was, incidentally, the most difficult to find, which shouldn't surprise you. But I felt the book would not be complete without one, and I owe much—that is everything but revelation—to dear, articulate Pauline, a grand presence on the golf links of the Southwest.

Yes, there are "different" types here, but even their samenesses lean toward individuality. They know the locations of the Bimbo bars, but they also know what they will and won't do when they get there. Each has her own structured precepts of what's right and what's wrong in this life style of playing the sports game. Yet, one rule of thumb, one prerequisite springs from each. Rosie, the big sister of professional football, expounds it with the most clarity: "I dig athletes because they're clean," she says. "They have to take a lot of showers. And so, as long as they're clean...."

Why not.

()

An eminent social psychologist in Berkeley, California, was no more willing to render value judgment on the nature of the Bimbos than I. Early in the research, however, I thought it might be pertinent to ask questions of someone who could help me ask questions of the Bimbos. The psychologist, a warm, kind, older man, was intrigued with the subject. He made no effort to hide his curiosity either. Together, we ferreted. Together, we decided that labels were not valid. He had notions, but placed no significance on them. What he offered were not theories but musings, yet thoughts to be shared by you, and me, and, because they're more entitled than the rest of us, the Bimbos. And so, for the consideration of all concerned, this bit of affectionate brainstorming from a good man not fearful of saying that he didn't know for sure:

"Does it, I wonder, belong with the bobby sox phenomenon? Do these women experience a sort of magic just, in effect, to touch the hem of a sports star's garment?

"The woman's deep feeling and interest in the sport is not all that important, perhaps. She must know just enough to make conversation with the athlete.

"Being with these women could be a kind of power thing for the athlete. Despite being great figures, they are still little boys and need to be taken care of. And, by the same token, the need to be seen with an athlete is kind of a childish thing for the woman. Call it participation in the glory. And it's rather an easy way to do it. You don't have to work very hard to achieve this participation. You don't have to be a star in *anything* yourself.

"Could it be that your Bimbos feel they don't have anything going for themselves? That they are women who are powerless and anonymous and obscure? Are they women who lack a sense of self-importance? Yet a woman who has the nerve to be picked up by a prominent figure?

"We would be wrong to use the term 'ego satisfaction' in connection with what they do. It would be more apt to say that these women have a need for self-esteem, that they are looking for a quick, easy way to boost their self-esteem, and that they achieve this boost by being close to what they consider to be greatness.

"And possibly, among some of the women, there may be a certain inclination toward masochism—enough self-hatred to degrade themselves. So that if a woman does degrade herself, she feels why not do it with a really important figure. This way, she can feed her masochism and her need for self-esteem at the same time. Bear in mind that it takes a certain amount of self-degradation to make your body available at a moment's notice. Yet, this is a thrilling experience for the woman.

"Connect it to the common human thrill. I think there have probably been more men than women who get satisfaction out of being close to greatness—shaking hands with someone of prominence, even being in the same room with an important figure. This is a common human thrill, and so the right spirit in which to view your women, your Bimbos, is that they are just people.

"Be kind to them. Don't put them down."

()

Two other tidbits from this consultation merit notation here:

1. The good doctor smiled as I discussed the lady in Missouri who dug umpires. "The umpire, the referee, the man who makes the calls in any sport is quite a father figure. He really has the power to make a final judgment."

2. "If you don't ask your women any other question, be sure to ask them if they have had better orgasms with an athlete."

All right. The last question is fair. Difficult for me to ask sometimes, but fair. And the answer always came easily, for the Bimbo was fascinated by the psychologist's fascination with her. She would listen, grin sort of sheepishly while summoning visions of orgasms past, and then ask me: "Better how? Better than with who? You mean, the best ever?"

Their final answers, if in context, can be found in their individual stories. If you seek a consensus, though, I can tell you that the Bimbos were uncomplaining about their orgasms with athletes. There may have been a "civilian" or two along the line who brought them off with more majestic bombardment, but they were hard-pressed to recall consistently *better* climaxes than those experienced with jocks. The good doctor's question thus led more to reverie than psychological solution.

As fumbling as I often was in coughing out the orgasm question, I never could bring myself to ask a Bimbo about her possible need for self-degrading sex. But usually, I didn't have to raise that issue. The women would tiptoe up to it themselves. Oh, not in those precise terms; they wouldn't say, "I must be inclined toward masochism, so that's why I screw around so much." But they would edge into personal inquiry—questioning motives, evaluating physical needs, pondering morality, justifying life style. The self-examination made them uneasy.

"I feel," more than one said after a taping session ended, "that I've just gone through a session with a psychiatrist." Or, "This is the first time I've really ever given much thought to what I've been doing." Shallow? Or a common self-avoidance?

You'll find general denial of the need for self-esteem, of any admission that, in the psychologist's words, "the need to be seen with an athlete is kind of a childish thing." The women describe this companionship as "fun" but never childish, although they agree with the doctor's hunch that "the athlete is a little boy who needs to be taken care of." The Bimbo sees the athlete as a child and herself as a woman, while the athlete sees himself as a man and the Bimbo as the child. The eye of the beholder theory at work, eh? Well, not always. There is one Bimbo, interviewed but unpublished here, who admitted she was "a spoiled little brat" who played with athletes—a married New York Met and an unmarried Detroit Lion simultaneously—because it was "fun" and because "I'm just hooked on sports and athletes." She had an opportunity to marry her ideal man but didn't only because he was from Nashville, Tennessee, "and there aren't any professional sports teams there."

Not every Bimbo is a sports nut. One will tell you that she went to games only to be polite to her fellow, that she paid attention to the progress of the game only when she heard her man's name announced. Another says she checks the box scores for the names of *her* men and no others. Then we have "The Little Yellow Butterfly" and Pauline, both of whom admit sexual stimulation over the mere observation of a pitcher's motion and golfer's swing, respectively. Still, all of them realize they must—as the doctor suggests—know just enough about sports to make conversation.

And what of the doctor's suggestion that they may be "powerless and anonymous and obscure" women? Claudia, an attractive model and actress, insists that she's as vital a human being as the next person—not necessarily better than anybody else, but definitely not worse. Mildred, our grandmother Bimbo, believes she elevated herself out of anonymity by diddling with football players for several years. Now, she says, she has spotted thousands of current anonymous, obscure women—the ones in the stands who would like to be laid by the football players they're watching. While they can only cheer, Mildred can recall orgasms.

Certainly a tough talker named Phyllis never has and never will feel anonymous or obscure. Powerless once maybe, because, as she tells us, she found herself trapped in a hotel filled with football players and couldn't find a ride home. Now that's powerlessness.

The Shirleys have become Shirleys by shedding anonymity and obscurity. And could they have reached their eminence if they lacked potency in the first place? You'll recall that the good doctor couldn't quite equate the level of "nerve" among the Bimbos with what he felt was their sense of personal inadequacy. Unresearched but justifiable ambivalence on his part; researched but justifiable ambivalence on mine. I mean, I could not picture a girl like Georgie, a Bimbo admittedly seeking escape from a mundane existence, summoning the courage to hustle the way she says she did. And I verified her story.

There is no accounting. But why should there be by anyone but the Bimbos themselves? I remember somebody saying a few paragraphs ago that the right spirit in which to view "your Bimbos" is that they are just people. So nobody put them down, you hear? The ladies will deal with themselves—if they wish to, when they wish to, if they indeed ever get around to self-confrontation at all. We don't have to put them in beakers or memory banks, and they can defy classification all they want. The Bimbos don't got to show us any stinkin' badges.

()

Jessica Mitford, who has written brilliantly about funerals and prisons, was asked in 1973 to become a lecturer in sociology at San Jose State University in California. At first, she was reluctant to accept the job. Ms. Mitford said she wasn't quite certain what "sociology" was. "But I talked with some of my colleagues-to-be at a cocktail party," she said, "and, I must say, they really didn't have a clue either."

It ain't, you see, nobody's business but their own.

Herb Michelson
Oakland and San Geronimo, California
1975

pre-game stuff

When I was a kid in Brooklyn, the girls were called Babes. But when you found out a girl could be had, she became a Bimbo.

...Garry Schumacher, retired baseball writer and publicist for the New York/San Franciso Giants; the man who ascribed "rhubarb" to a fuss on the field.

Why do I screw around so much on the road? Just to relax, I guess. That more than anything else. All that dead time. Nothing to do. You can see a lot of movies, and I've done that. But there's so many movies now that make you horny. When I first got into the majors, there were four or five guys on my team who were always chasing on the road. I mean, they never got any sleep. Everybody used to go sneaking around to get laid in those days. But now there's so much of that kind of thing going on, there's no need to hide it. I never screw around when my club is home, or during the off-season. Why, during the winter I even give up smoking and drinking. In the off-season, I never have any idle time. And I think every ballplayer is the same way. It's when you don't have anything to do that you get in trouble.... One of baseball's best pitchers. Married.

Would I get as much stuff if I was just a traveling salesman? No, sir. It's not advertised that a traveling salesman is coming to town.

...An American Leaguer. Married.

the basic bimbo

marianne... *twenty-seven years old, blonde, five foot one, one hundred twenty five pounds. Outdoorsey cute. By her own estimate has slept with "around three hundred pro athletes over a seven-year period. Give or take a few." Daughter of a high-ranking, Southern California Navy officer. Majored in science at Long Beach State University, worked as a barber. At sixteen was fixed up by her sister with several California Angel baseball players. "I never screwed any of them then," she says. "I was scared of them. They were so forward. Animals, most of them." Played around during the four-year marriage "except while I was pregnant and when the two kids were really little. Just once or twice a month. It made life more exciting." Gregarious. "It's so easy to meet people. I'll talk to anybody with a nice personality. I just meet people—airport, supermarkets. Anywhere." Gives out her phone number "a lot." Had no phone at the time of this interview. Expressed abiding need to be satisfied sexually, once worried about possibility of being a nymphomaniac so went to a psychiatrist "three or four times. He said there was nothing wrong with me. He told me he thought I was superstable and that it was silly for me to pay him any more. That was a couple of years ago. I haven't gone back, and I haven't changed."*

I was in a bar and this golfer was with another girl I knew at the time just kind of casually. She introduced us. Oh, and if you don't mind, I'll just call him Mister B. Okay? We sat and chitchatted for maybe two or three hours over a couple drinks, and he asked me very nicely if I would care to come and see him play golf sometime. Or would I want to play golf with him? I told him I wasn't a very good golfer, that I had only played spontaneous, you know, about maybe four or five times. And he said that maybe he could give me some pointers on golf and we could have a good time. We did this once and got to like each other.

He's in his early forties. A very nice, very pleasant man. I knew he was married and the whole bit. I always ask beforehand—just to see how honest they are. Because a lot of them will lie. Anyway, we had a nice time playing golf, and he asked me if I would want to come to the next tournament he was playing at, and I said yes, that I thought it would be very interesting. Except the place was really too inconvenient. But later he called me and said there was another tournament not very far away, and did I want him to pick me up or meet him there. I said I would be very happy to meet him up there, which I did.

There wasn't any doubt why he wanted me to come there. I knew what it was. I hadn't slept with him before, but I liked him as a person. I knew we'd get together. There'd be something wrong if we didn't. He was very confident over the phone. You just assume you're gonna be three days together with one man in his place, away from your home, and that of course you're gonna sleep together. It didn't bother me. I had an interest going. And I'm sure he did, too.

He sublet a condominium from a friend that was right on the course. And we stayed there. It was beautiful, absolutely gorgeous. The first day I got there it was very lonely and boring because he was playing golf and had a lot of business people around him. So I took it upon myself to kind of show myself around. And I met a lot of people that showed me around. There were some girls who I guess were doing the same thing up there as me. I didn't ask them. I don't pry. But I'm assuming. I played a few sets of tennis with some girls there. And then my golfer and I ate lunch together. And then we ate dinner together and sat there at the cocktail lounge at the golf club and had a few drinks and talked, getting to know each other. Then we went back to the condominium because he had to play golf again the next day. And we slept together that first night. It was very nice.

I don't have any expectations about different kinds of athletes. Just by talking to them you can tell about their moral concepts and hangups and inhibitions. I don't really think I have any inhibitions. I trace over a lot of things myself. I don't go in for gang-bangs or orgies or three men on me at once or anything, but I don't think that's an inhibition or a hangup, or even a definite moral code. I just like to service one person.

Once, though, my girlfriend Norma and I were going to try and take on one guy together, just to see. We got wiped out one night and went all over the place looking for some guy to pick up and blow his mind. But we couldn't find anybody suitable for both of us.

Norma kept saying, "How about him?" And I'd say he looked too slobby. Or I'd point out a guy and she'd say he looked too straight.

Norma and I are like that. We're close. I don't know what we would have done if we'd picked up a guy. But I'm sure he would have helped. We would probably have played it by ear and giggled a lot and said to him, "What do you want first? Front or back or bottom or...?"

It depends on the guy a lot, you know. He might have a special liking to the way I kiss more so than what Norma does, and he might like intercourse with her more so than with me. So that's why you'd have to play it by ear. Someday we're definitely gonna do it, as soon as we find a prospect we both agree on.

With Mister B. I had a beautiful sexual time at the golf tournament. He was a very gentle, very soft, slow-moving man. He doesn't overexert himself. He's a very nice lover— calm, mellow, enjoyable. He doesn't beat your brains out in bed. I really enjoyed him. A beautiful sexual relationship to me is one where I don't have to completely overexert myself. Like the first night I was with B. I can remember bits and pieces of him saying, "My God, you just turn me on," or something like: "You feel so good."

I would say a woman is supposed to make a man feel good. And he would say, "But there's so many women that don't. There's so many lazy women that lay there and expect the world to come to them." He said some very nice things to me.

I went down on him the first night we were at the tournament and he said that he just couldn't handle it, that it was too much for him and that he wanted to satisfy me. And I said that I satisfy myself by knowing that the man is completely taken care of; that when I leave a man he has a nice thought about every little bit of time that we spent together—even if he's exhausted. And he said it was, you know, the ultimate; it was beautiful. He did finally let me go down on him.

I've never had a man tell me no. When you're having a sexual affair with a man you don't just jump on him and go down the first thing. You find out a little bit about how he moves, how he works, if he's a hard screw or a gentle, loving, warm, sincere man, or if he's just a guy after a piece of ass. You know: Stick it in, get off, and wham-bam-thank-you-ma'am. You find these things out as a person, and this is what I did with B.

I tried to find out how he works in bed as a man, as a lover, and by doing this I didn't even ask on the second night when I went down on him. And by then he didn't turn me away because I guess I approached him the right way. I'm very adventurous.

The first night is like experimenting. You don't know what you're in for. You really don't know how his endurance goes, how long he can keep an erection going, or if he's so worked up he's going to ejaculate right off the bat. You don't know these things, so this is what you find out.

The second night you take all consideration of the first night, compile your information together and weigh it and make your move. The second night he loves to be touched as a man; he doesn't like you just to lay beside him. He likes me to rub his back, to stroke his chest and kiss him on the chest and the nose and all over his neck and arms and all. And we talk while we're doing this, you know, and I just seem to work my way down.

And when I work my way down to where I'm supposed to be, B. puts his hand on my shoulder, you know, and his finger in my ear, just playing around and told me: "My God, I don't know if I can hold off. I don't know if I can handle it. It feels so good." So you have to play these things by ear.

I'll never forget him saying to me: "For such a little lady, you are a lot of woman." He said he underestimated me. And I told him that I thought that was a compliment, and I was real happy.

The second day of the tournament I started to walk the course. I told him I'd been kind of lonesome and bored being out there all by myself. So he got me an electric cart, and I followed him for a while until I got tired of driving around in circles by myself—because he was so busy while he was playing golf and so businesslike. Golf is life in a game; you can't bother him no matter how lonesome you are.

So I left the cart with someone else and just walked around looking like I knew what I was doing. Every time there was a hole in one or birdie or something, I was trying to look like I was on top of what golf is all about. Which I'm not. I'm not too into golf itself. But the third day I walked the course with with him, and because I was thirsty and it was a little warm, I started drinking. Had a heck of a good time; got wiped out. A few of the other golfers made some friendly kind of moves about picking me up. I didn't take it as a definite make, but quite a few times a lot of them put their arms around me and asked if I wouldn't want to caddy for them, or, why didn't I come over to their place and leave Mister B. alone.

I saw some lovely models around, and a couple of stewardesses. And some older women that were really beautiful—not only nice looking but very pleasant and personable. There were so many stray girls I wouldn't dare put them all together with all the golfers. But I know that not too many of the golfers' wives were around because one night I saw a lot of pairing.

We were all having a few drinks at the cocktail lounge at Silverado and everybody put their tables together and had a chitchat. You know. Golf, or just world affairs, or whatever. Of course there was dancing. One person would ask a girl at this table to dance, and everybody would join everybody else. There were some stray girls that had come in from the golf course. I'm positive that they were picked up the second night. These girls didn't look any different to me than gals I've seen at baseball and football bars, although I think golfers are a little different from other athletes.

I think they work harder at their game. A baseball player is a baseball player. He plays baseball in the afternoon or the night and then he just parties, parties, parties. A golfer is more tense. Golf is his life. He devotes himself body and soul to that game, especially to that particular tournament he's in.

I understood what B. was up there for. I couldn't ask him to leave his golf game for me just because I've come up to see him. But I did once ask him why he had me come up. And he said, "When I see something I like, I go after it. Even if I'm with another lady at the time." And that's what he did.

He asked me if I had ever dated another golfer, and I told him yes. He wanted to know who, and I told him I didn't think it was proper for me, you know, to start mentioning names because he wouldn't want me to ask about his girlfriends. And he laughed. He said, "All right. We'll drop it."

He did very good in the tournament. I think it was second. Second or third. It wasn't very bad. He was a little upset with the way he was playing, but I thought he did fantastic considering the other people in the tournament. But everybody does that. If you don't win, you don't feel like

you've done your best. After this tournament he was flying to another state, I think it was Florida, and he asked me if I'd be able to go. Would I have babysitting problems or anything? And I told him that I thought the three days and two nights were very lovely, I enjoyed myself. I thanked him. Every so often I hear from him. And if I want to talk to him, I can make a phone call. It's not hard to get invited places if you know how to do it.

()

At this little local tournament one of the pro football players put on, I was a hostess and got to meet this golfer from out of town. Let's just say his name is Jay. Okay? We just started talking at a party after the trophies were given out, and I ended up with him that night. He was great fun. Crazy, but fun. We got along well, and I slept with him a couple of times. He asked me to come to a tournament in Southern California and spend a few days. I had just gotten a new car and needed to put some miles on it to break it in. And a couple of girlfriends wanted to go with me. He said he could fix them up and that the three of us should drive there.

He gave me a gas credit card, but I wouldn't take it. I didn't want to be obligated about sending it back to him. So I took care of the gas and let him take care of everything else. I did get a flat tire, though, and he bought me a new tire. It was a factory tire, but I think it was a reject on a new car. And he paid for the new tire with his credit card.

He set up the hotel for us and all. There was one room for the three of us girls with two double beds. The whole atmosphere around the tournament was really just beautiful: Good weather and private clubs and swimming, and he took us all out to dinner. Great time.

Jay had an apartment of some kind in a sort of beach and tennis club. A big complex. I spent the night there, but there were a couple of phone calls that really made me stop and think. I had asked him if he was married, and he was very honest and said yes, he was. I had no idea where his wife was or if this was his permanent residence. And he told me not to answer the phone.

One call seemed to upset him—I don't know who it was. I asked him if he wanted to take me back to the hotel, and he said, "Oh no. Don't worry about it. It was nothing." And I said, "Well, it must be something because whoever the phone call was from you got really uptight." And he told me that it was a girl that found out I was there and that she was planning on seeing him, but there was a little mixup. He said he'd take care of it all later. I never found out who the girl was. She never approached me or anything.

But a lot of women look at you, even the barmaids, the cocktail waitresses at some of these private clubs who must know his wife or know people he runs around with. They looked at me and my girlfriends as if to say: "Well, I wonder where they were imported from?" That hadn't happened to me at the earlier tournament. And you know how very married Mister B. is. But there in Southern California I got an uneasy feeling and I told Jay this. He said if there was anything he could do to make me more comfortable to please let him know.

He introduced my girlfriends to some guys—one of them a really famous foreigner. I knew my friends would be fixed up because Jay said there would be plenty of men around and that the girls could take their pick.

He said, "We'll have the golfers stand in line and the girls can go eenie, meenie, minie, mo." The girls were quite willing to do this. Anything to get away for a weekend and have fun. With no obligations, no ties, you know. They enjoyed themselves. One of the girls stayed in our hotel room with the foreigner, and the other went somewhere with her golfer. I really can't remember his name. Kind of sandy-colored hair. What was his name? Both girls had a gas, really enjoyed themselves.

When we were driving back, we all kind of put our information together. They asked me if I liked Jay, and I told them that he was a hell of a man. He had given me a few phone numbers to contact him in different places where the pro golf tour would be and told me he'd help me get there if I could make it. He was very happy with me. I've seen him maybe three or four times since then. But just at my home. I'd rather him come to me and see me. Tournaments are boring. They are. You can't get wild or obnoxious. You've got to be very quiet, too.

Just like at my first golf tournament, a lot of the married golfers weren't with their wives. But who am I to say, you know? I don't know a married man that doesn't play around. I never felt immoral when I played around while I was married. Not now, either. I felt a little guilty in my married days, but not immoral. I had a few guilt feelings wondering if I might get caught.

Once the wife of a Washington Senators pitcher I was going out with found out about us. I'd been fixed up on a blind date with him by a relief pitcher I knew. And the Senator and I hit it off fantastic. We fell in love, is what we did. He was just married to a stewardess who was pregnant and they had to get married and the whole bit. I kept seeing him. She left to visit her family in the East one winter, and I met the Senator in Minnesota to snowmobile for two weeks. Flew there with my kids.

Well, somebody must have said something or other because Mrs. Senator found out and confronted her husband with this. He said, "Hey, I don't know what you're talking about. It must be some other baseball player. It's not me. I have nothing to do with that kind of stuff."

Lied his way out of it, I guess. Mrs. Senator found out again that we continued to see each other, and I got a nasty letter from her. Real nasty. It was a real cutie. I have no idea how she got my address. She called me a home wrecker and the whole bit, you know. A slut and that kind of stuff.

It really made me mad because I can't help it that he fell in love with me. I mean, it's a sad thing, especially for a married man. But I can't help it, you know. He fell in love with me on his own feelings, and I'm happy he did because I

11   *marianne*

enjoyed every minute of it. I love him still. He's a beautiful man. Divorced now.

You know, I've never really been worried that some people might look on me as a whore or something nasty like that. I've never, never felt like that myself. You show me a woman that doesn't screw, okay? A single woman who is twenty-seven years old, divorced, very worldly—like myself—who goes out in the public, meeting the public, especially in my old barber's job. I work with nothing but men so I had the opportunity all day long, every day, seven days a week if I wanted to.

Show me a woman that's put in my position that doesn't do the things I do, and then I'll feel guilty. She'd have to be mighty virtuous and mighty saintly before I'd feel immoral, guilty, a whore, a slut, or anything. I am an average person just like everybody else. I have a sex drive just like every other woman. The way I go about getting myself serviced or finding my own involvements with men is maybe different from everybody else, but they still do it. Even married women.

I think I have a bigger sex drive, only because it's harder for me to be satisfied. I'm satisfied only about fifty percent of the time. I'd like it to be about one hundred percent. But half the time isn't bad for a woman. I consider myself lucky. I'd like it to be more, but fifty percent of the time I guess is better than average. I love every minute of being a woman. I've conquered the ups and downs of being mature and immature. Sexually, too. The accomplishments that I've made I'm very proud of. I think I've done a good deal. I've done well being a woman, and I don't want to be anything else. I like it. I like being the gentle, the feminine, the little fragile type.

()

I feel sorry for the wives of pro athletes. As much as I mess around with athletes—and I'd say that around seventy five percent of them are married—I get flown everywhere and get presents and cards and letters and money spent on me. And I have to wonder what these guys do for their wives.

I like very few of the wives. They make me feel uncomfortable, and they have this nose-up-in-the-air attitude about them; that they're so much better than I am. I don't think anybody is better than anybody else. Most of them are very snobbish, very cold. There are a few that are very friendly and wonderful people, but they started out like I did—playing the baseball game and accidentally marrying a ballplayer. And all of them know their husbands play around. You don't have to be a baseball player to play around.

There are men like my father, who plays around on my mother. Sure, my mother knows. But she's been married to him thirty-seven years. Sure, he's treated her every bit like a queen on a pedestal, provided very well for her. So what more could she ask? You can't keep a man from playing around.

Marriage is a farce to me. The old marriage-type thing, the very beautiful bond that two people have together between them is no longer. Marriage today is nothing more than two people being able to live together with no guilt. That's all. A man does what he wants to do, and a woman can't keep him from it. When she starts pressuring him, she loses him. The wife who doesn't question her husband about what he does on the road trips will keep her husband for a lifetime. She'll find out in the long run that she's made it, that those years of feeling a little bit unsure and neglected are worth it. But too few women are strong enough to do this.

And I've seen some athletes' wives who play around too. Maybe it's because they know their husbands are doing the same thing. It's not wrong. Not at all. I feel that if a woman is not totally happy with the man she is married to or living with, then she better seek companionship outside her home. It solves a lot of problems in her own mind, and it makes her a better person to find out what these problems are, why these conflicts are in her mind.

13   *marianne*

I know myself, when I was married, I thought that maybe just going out with somebody else would either prove to me that I loved my husband much more than I thought, or that I didn't love him. And there's only one way to find out, and it's not to get a divorce. If you want to keep your marriage strong and save the marriage, you have to go out and have an affair to see what you want.

Freedom is something people don't know about if they're married. So they should try to be free—for just one moment, one night, one hour—and see if that's what they need. They piece these things together in their mind and find out that either it was wrong being married, or it was right. And they're going to stop and settle down and think about nothing but pleasing their husbands. They'll find out that outside men bore them, that they are nothing, that what they already have means much more to them than what they could go out and find.

()

Sure it's possible to compare the different kinds of athletes in bed. I think every woman has a grading system. I am a body woman. Okay? I like a man who is physically fit, with a nice body. A physique that—even when he's well-dressed, concealing all—is in tune, turns me on. I'm not talking about muscles. Musclebound people don't interest me. I just have this thing about a nice, physical body.

I don't like men who are overweight. I don't like super-skinny men. I don't like short men. Or stocky men. I just have this ideal person who is six foot two. Six foot and above, okay? And because I'm blonde and have light, gray-green eyes and was married to a blonde with blue eyes, I seem to be attracted to dark, brunette-type men with very beautiful white teeth and smiles, big smiles. That turns me on.

I don't care what he looks like, if he's got really straight, beautiful, white teeth and a big smile. I go gung-ho. I'm a physical hygiene nut: a super-nut. If they're slobbish, you can just forget it. I just tell them to get away from me. I can't stand it. And this is another reason I run with athletes. Ninety-nine percent of your athletes are super-clean men; they have to be. They're checked frequently. They have to shower at least twice a day because of the way they work out. Their bodies are in tone and firm. No matter if they wear glasses and have fuzzy hair, they're usually nice looking. They dress well and they're clean.

I can't stand unclean people. I like to wear jeans and a T-shirt and go barefoot and walk along the beach, but I know I'm clean. And I like to know that the person I'm walking with—I don't care if he has cutoffs and a tank shirt on—is clean also. And I never run into problems with athletes being slobs. None of them are. I've never had VD. Oh, God help me. I've never contracted anything, knock on wood. I don't know why. I must have been lucky.

Out of all the sports and of all the men I date which is, you know, every sport in the world—I don't care if they're ping-pong players, you know—out of all this I think that baseball players are the best in bed. For me. Baseball players make the best lovers. I don't know why, I can't say.

Football players are big, beautiful brutes that don't know how to handle their bodies in bed. They're lovely people. They're much more intelligent than baseball players. They've been to college. They've just got a lot more on the ball. They can carry conversations and are much more worldly. They can talk about almost anything. But with a baseball player, sometimes you can get hung up just talking about baseball and that's it. In bed though, it's different.

I have dated fifteen million football players and I love them all. They're all beautiful, dear friends of mine, but maybe only ten of them are good bed partners. Ten out of the fifteen million. That's bad odds. The reason being that most of them are big men. Heavy. They're big-built. And usually when you find a man which I would consider a football player type—six foot one, 210 pounds, you know, a fifty-six chest or whatever you want—well, he usually doesn't have anything. And if he has anything to work with, he's heavy and he's lazy. They're just not good lovers.

It's not the weight alone that bothers me. If a man is too heavy for little me, I'll just switch over. I'll lay on him so that he can get my weight. There's a lot of men that like me on top of them, but I never come when I'm on top. Never. There's not enough movement for me, and I need the stroking. With me on top, I'm usually working him. And that's all.

I think maybe I did climax once on top with this guy who used to pitch for the Texas Rangers, but that's only because he's so hung it doesn't matter what position you're in. You feel every bit of him, and he makes sure you do.

But the penis size isn't that important a thing for me. It really isn't. Some of my girlfriends strive for a well-hung man, but you never know until you get in bed with them.

I'll tell you one thing: It's not a question of how big it is, it's a question of how big a woman can get it. A man can get what he thinks is a full erection with one woman, and he can blast her right off him with another. It depends. It's all mental. It really is with a man. And if you work that man up to the biggest he's ever been, well, then, he's gonna feel like a telephone pole inside of you.

Every man wants to have a little bit more than the average. If I were to line up two football players, two baseball players, two hockey players, and two basketball players in a row and the only thing that was showing was from the chest to the knees, you know the genital area only, I'd probably run to the basketball player because they're huge men. Huge, but beautiful physical specimens. Muscular, trim, masculine. They're just beautiful men. They are.

But almost any athlete is better in bed than the average man. They're out making the sex trip a lot more. I guess it's more practice. They work a lot harder at it because they lay so many different women, you know, so many days a week and in so many different towns. And they learn techniques, different techniques. They're physically and sexually mature. But not humanly mature.

They're spoiled; they're moody. They want to be pampered and fondled. They're like little boys that need a mother to take care of them. Many of them are giant assholes. But physically and sexually they're well-equipped. And I know that if I were a male, I would be right in there with them. This is where I fit in as a woman, in the same category that they do. I guess that's why I run with them.

I know that when I'm out with a well-known athlete people are staring. I feel that they envy me and that they are a little jealous of what I might have that they don't have because I'm with someone special and they're not. But that doesn't make me feel important. I feel important just being myself. I consider myself important. So I don't need a man by my side who's of any certain status.

I dress well. I dress to be noticed. When you're in a group of people, in a bar that's crowded with lovely girls, a man will pick out a girl who is dressed what you call flamboyantly. I don't mean cheaply. I mean, like, in very good taste. Sometimes just a certain type of jewelry.

Like take a basic outfit, a very nice black velvet backless top with black and white things and striped pants. It sounds sexy because it is. But if you wanted to be noticed, all you would have to do is wear a very, large, silver necklace—like, say, charging lions in a row. Something that's big and noticeable. And maybe very large earrings. And shoes. Like, say a look that has a little class to it. Maybe a silver buckle that shows.

Your makeup, everything has to coordinate, and I dress this way to coordinate everything so that when I walk into a place at least if they don't say, "Isn't that a beautiful outfit," they can say, "That young lady has good taste in clothes."

A man notices right off. Many, many times over they'll say, "Check out the way that chick is dressed." You know. Even if they don't like my face or the way my figure is, or anything, they can say, "Look at that outfit." And time after time, men have told me the reason I stand out in a place is the way I dress. Heads turn. And it gives me a chance to look at their faces, see what kind of eyes they have, if they have a smiling face and nice, bright white smiles. Or a slobby look.

I'm very hair conscious because I was a barber, so I notice men's hair a lot. If a man has a beautiful, well-cut head of hair, I stare. Not because I'm unkind or trying to put the make on him. Just curiosity because I'm wondering about the barber, about the haircut fitting the man's head, about what the man would look like with another kind of haircut.

And a man is the same way. He looks at a woman and thinks to himself: She wears her makeup very clean and very well put together. It's not heavy and it's not too natural. Her hair is not too bouffant and not too plain but it's a cute style and fits her face. And her clothes fit the woman. I know men say this to themselves. I've asked many times, so I know. If I have an outfit I'm not too sure of, I'll wear it in a subdued sort of atmosphere and find out what kind of reaction I get from different people. And if it's a good reaction, then I'll wear it places athletes are.

This is what I do. I just like to feel sort of special, and I do. I like myself. I'm honest. I'm responsible. And I'm super-independent. I feel like I'm a good person. I don't intentionally hurt anybody, and so when I go out I want people to feel the same way I feel. I'm totally secure as a person and in my mind also.

My ex-husband pays child support and alimony. And of course when I work, I make a lot of money as a barber. Barbers make good money. And then my mom and dad are always showering me with something. So I'm secure. And I guess I'm spoiled. I am used to nice places, people who are impressive, who are very free spending money, who are not afraid of tipping and things like this.

You take your average non-athlete man, who we'll say is middle class. The reason why he is middle class and has a little money is because he doesn't spend freely often. Believe me, they don't.

I met somebody who is a hundred-fifty-thousand dollar-a-year financial status type. I would call him very wealthy, okay? And he does not spend money freely. He is so tight, he squeaks when he walks. And he's a big bore to be out with.

When I go out myself, I spend money as a person. And athletes are like that too. That's why they're fun to be with. But unless I'm emotionally involved with a non-athlete, I get bored hearing about his personal financial problems.

If I am involved, why, then, of course I want to be a part of that. I want to help, be right in there. I'll scrimp and scrounge and start a budget going if that's going to help him out. But if I'm not involved, I don't want it. I want to enjoy myself in luxury because very shortly, being as I'm twenty-seven years old, I can feel it coming—I'm going to want to stay home and save money and do things in the future for myself and for my children. So right now I live for every moment of today.

I'm not the least bit tired of playing the pro sports circuit. I keep wanting more. I'd like to have a different athlete beside me every night of the week. Which is impossible. And he'd have to do more for me than just give me an orgasm. I'm not just a person who goes out and finds a body and takes him home and tries to satisfy him.

I mean, I'm not that satisfied in bed unless there's a mental and emotional bond going also. And I think that's why I don't get satisfied a lot. Because a lot of times I find a person who's geared to my level mentally and not sexually, or sexually geared to my level and not mentally. See? I've got to try to reach this happy medium.

It's never been a case of going to bed with an athlete just because there's nothing else to do. That's not helping me, and it's not helping him. Very rarely have I ever done it. When I have, it's usually been the case of a girlfriend needing to be with someone else. And I've been thrown together with somebody that really bores me to death, but I'm not gonna blast her plans, you know. I'm gonna make sure she has a good time because this is something she's been looking forward to. So I'll do anything I can to make sure that she's happy. Even at the risk of having a meaningless lay. I've done that a lot of times for my girlfriends. And I, in turn, have had them do that for me, too. I'm pretty sensitive, you know.

()

I live in an old Victorian mansion that's decorated totally Marianne. In my bedroom I have a big king size waterbed with black and white fur rugs on the floor, zebra-skinned. And I have a white fur bedspread with a canopy top. It's very sensuous. I have mirrors...it's a sin den is what it is. The first time this pitcher from Texas came over to my place and saw my bedroom, he showed me pictures of his own apartment and told me his waterbed had a heater and a vibrator and was totally equipped. He wondered how much my bed stuff cost, and we compared prices. He said his waterbed was custom-made, so his cost a lot more than mine. We were in the bedroom talking until five o'clock in the morning. The sun was gonna come up, and I was exhausted and he was the starting pitcher the next day, in the second game of a double-header. So I asked him how the hell he was going to pitch after sitting up and talking all night.

He said, "Don't worry about it. We do it all the time."

When I'm going to spend the night with an athlete, I like to go to my house and not their hotel, because usually they're all roomed up. They come in pairs. I like my house. I'm comfortable in my own bedroom. I can sleep in my bed. Most of the time my children aren't there. If I know I'm gonna be out with a ballplayer all night, I take the kids to my mother's, or get a baby-sitter. And if the kids are home when I have a player in my bedroom, it's nothing to worry about. I've never yet in my life met a ballplayer who gets up early in the morning.

Usually if we've been out drinking most of the night, he'll stay sound asleep in my bed. I'll close my bedroom door just like nothing's happened. I'll get up, fix my children's breakfast, get them dressed and send them off to school. And by the time they come home, the house is the same. They never know a person's been there.

There's no problem. I have no guilt about it. If my kids ask me a question, I answer it very honestly. They do not disrespect me. They're not maladjusted. They're fantastic. People will tell you my kids are groovy. They're good kids. I make a point of taking them out at least one night every week. Just the three of us.

()

I enjoy going to games. If I've been with an athlete who really, totally interests me and I'd like to see him again, then I'll follow up on him. I'll read the paper. I'll listen for names on the news. And read sports books or anything I can get my hands on.

I sometimes ask them for addresses so I can write them. I send them an appropriate card. You know, a funny card or a dirty card, or just a misleading note. Sometimes I'll get quite a few responses from these letters and cards and things. The players enjoy it.

One pitcher once told me, "The happiest thing for a baseball player is to come back home after meeting some girl—who he's maybe spent a night or two nights with—without much time to get to know her—but still to know there's an interest there. And you think about these girls. You think from time to time wherever you are, gee, I sure wish there was another Marianne around."

It's heartwarming.

the grandmother

millie... *forty-eight years old; five feet two inches tall, one hundred five pounds...grandmother of three ...divorced after twenty-four years of marriage...past seven years has been a sexual partner for numberless National Football League players....says she's played three roles to these athletes: housemother, dating agency, physical contributor...feels these experiences gave her "the youth I missed"...tries to play the clown when she's with the players, although "underneath I'm very deep"...has done secretarial work...father "always dreamed that I would get to know just one football player"...was introduced to first player by her husband...first player introduced her to second, then second to third, with whom she had first N.F.L. sex ...goes to all the games. "When I sit in the stands at a game and watch all those people cheering, I figure there are about three thousand women in the stadium who are saying to themselves that they'd like to be in bed with this player or that player. And I want to say to those women: 'Yell your bloody lungs out, because I've slept with most of these beautiful bastards out there on the field.' I've been there, and you can't knock that. It's a good, good feeling." Football sex days, she says, are confined to Tuesdays, Wednesdays and Thursdays, because Sunday is "game and family day"; Monday is "rest day—they play golf or something"; Friday is "a sort of stay-at-home type of night"; Saturday nights "they're always locked up"....*

22

I think I'm known as a Football Annie, or an Athlete Annie.
Some athletes have, I think, used me over the years, just to
plain *use* me. Others, I think, have liked me.

I guess most of the time I don't mind being known as a
Football Annie. But sometimes it bothers me badly. It didn't
the first two or three years. I mean, I was a virgin when I got
married, then I had a bad marriage sexually. So when I got
away from it—and I had been totally frustrated—I was like a
kid let loose again. I wanted to live. And I really lived.

But all of a sudden, about a year or two ago, I had this sort
of rude awakening. I felt that I was being used by a lot of the
football fellows. Not by all of them; I could single out five or
six that are warm, beautiful human beings. But when I
finally realized what I was doing and how I was being
treated, I didn't like it at all. So that's why this last season
I've slowed down about two hundred percent.

The older players are calling me still, but not the newer,
younger ones. They're an entirely different breed. The new
ones are most self-centered. I don't think they sit back and
think of other peoples' emotions—that I'm human, that I
have feelings, that I can get hurt, that I may have had a past
that's made me the way I am today.

All they think about is themselves, and doing that they
forget how easily one play could wipe them out, and they
could be a nothing. Then if they were ever really looking for a
true friend, they would have one in me. But they don't
realize any of this.

()

I think this is the first year that I have to say—and I'll use
a baseball term rather than football—that I struck out.

Age is finally catching up with me. In looks. I have to be
honest with myself. I have to take a big, long look in my
mirror and admit that I'm not the glamour girl that these

23   *millie*

young, good-looking chicks are that are around and available to the athletes. Some of these younger chicks can offer the same thing to a player as I can, or the fellows *think* they can. The players would rather chance that than be with somebody who's a little bit older.

Sure, I always was competing with the glamour girls. But in my first few years in football, I was younger and I looked younger. Still, I don't feel I look old, and I don't feel I'm a has-been by a longshot, but I think that I've just suddenly caught up to my age.

I know I said before that I'm backing off. But I think I have to admit that I've been forced to back off. I've now reached another step or another crossroad in my life. Where am I going to go? What am I going to do? I'm going to have to make some decisions, and make them quickly.

I don't ever want to give up football, that's not what I'm saying. But I have to find something else.

Still, I'll miss having all those guys. Physically and emotionally. I think I have the mental contact with them now, stronger than I ever did, but the physical contact is very negative right now. I can honestly say that I'm hornier now than I have been in years. I still have a few that come to see me, but it's not like it used to be. That's the whole thing.

After you have sex so often with so many good-looking men, it's hard to lose that. I'm not a jealous person, but in a funny way I'm envious of the younger girls today. Sure, I can sit back and say that I was there once. I'm not vindictive toward them or anything.

I made a statement at one point when I was about to get a divorce. I prayed then that maybe God would give me a few years of what I'd missed. And I said then that if and when the time came that I ever had to go, I'd always be thankful for whatever I had—but to *please* give it to me. Well, I feel I've had it by now. I don't feel it's over with, but there's less of it.

So I can sit back now and say: okay, I was there for a few years.

And I've seen this happen to other women. I have one
girlfriend who stepped completely aside from football after a
while. All her dates now are completely unrelated to sports.
Same thing with a couple other girlfriends of mine. We all
used to go around together. Now we've all sort of, uh, you
know....

()

After I started my first football affair—and he was very
warm and patient with me—a reputation developed for me.
Once that reputation got started, it went into the locker
room and got passed from fellow to fellow. Each one I was
with just kept building that reputation for me. I would play a
little sexual game with them; like, I knew more than I
actually did. Still, I would wait for them to make the first
move and then kind of take the lead from them after I
realized what they wanted. And sometimes, I just kind of
faked it a little bit—pretending that I enjoyed it more than I
did, because some of them weren't as good as they thought
they were. But you could never break down the male
egotism, so you had to let them think they were great.

From each one, though, I learned something: his art of
making love, his little special ways. At the beginning, I
learned about the foreplay. I learned that I liked to be kissed
and caressed, and whether they also wanted to be kissed and
caressed or just jump into bed and get their rocks off. One
fellow paid me a very high compliment when he told me he
thought my rhythm was so good. And than made me stop to
think that I had never even thought about my rhythm. But
then when I was with the *next* fellow, I became aware of my
rhythm. I wanted to keep a nice, steady pace for him. If one
fellow thought I was so good at it, I guess I just thought I
should keep it up.

And I think I've helped some of them along the way, too,
after I began to learn about sex. Some of them would just

think they were playing with you correctly, so I'd make them put their hands on my breasts and make them think, gee, I was so excited by that. So they began to learn to do this.

I had another player who was, oooh, not too rough, but he bit a little. I told him, "Don't do that. That isn't nice. Kiss instead." And so he did. I think it was just a case of us learning about each other.

But I never have become mechanical about sex. I found each new fellow a big challenge and a lot of fun.

()

The first time I went to bed with a football player, it was all set up by one of the other players who was just a real close friend and an awfully nice fellow. He told me that this player would be waiting for me at a bar. I didn't go for a few minutes because I was really scared about doing it. I knew what would happen if I met the player at the bar. I was thinking how big he was and how little I was, and for that short time while I was thinking about it I was just plain scared. I mean, I knew what would happen after I met him.

Down deep, though, I knew this was what I was looking for. Yet the first time makes you a little apprehensive. But I finally did go to meet him, and I was right—he was huge. We talked for a little while in the bar, then walked out to his car, and he drove to his apartment. We talked there, and the next thing I knew we were in bed.

By that point, I was more scared of myself than him— because at that time, even though I was separated, I hadn't been out with too many men. And my divorce still wasn't finalized. I guess I lived in the dark ages-type of world, worried about what would happen if I got found out, because I was still legally married. And I didn't really know that much about sex. I felt completely and totally inadequate when it came to sex.

But the way it turned out, this player taught me more about sex than any man I've ever been with. That first night he said to me, "You're a very warm woman, but you've got a great big fence around you, and I'm going to do everything I can to knock it down."

He didn't teach me about sex in a way that a child learns to read a book. You know: Run, John, Run. It was just that he was patient and understanding; most men would have figured, well, she's kind of bad, I don't want her again. Instead of him saying that, he told the players about me, and the other guys told other guys. And my sex life just kept building.

When I look back upon that first night, I know I must have been just terrible sexually. I mean, I didn't know what I was doing really. It wasn't that I just laid back and waited for things to happen, but these football fellows were just so much more worldly and manly than anything I'd ever experienced before. I'd never had anything like that in all the years of my marriage.

There was always a little bit of foreplay in sex when I was married, but then it always ended so fast. And when it was over, I always had the feeling I still wanted more. But I didn't realize what the *more* was that I wanted. I'd hold onto my ex-husband after we'd had sex and tell him, "I love you."

He would always say, "Aw, I gotta get up and clean up now." And he'd leave. I can remember crying in bed when he'd do that. I realize now that it was frustration that was making me cry—because I wasn't satisfied. In twenty-four years of marriage, I had very few orgasms. Very few.

But these football fellows were able to bring out all the many more orgasms I was supposed to have felt, or had, in all those years before. Maybe all those years of frustration brought out the meanness in me when I was married.

This first football player just showed me how to relieve all that frustration. He played with me like a woman, both before and after the sex. He didn't leave me the minute the sex was over. Just being able to lay there and hold onto somebody after it was over was a great thing for me, because this had never happened with my ex-husband. All the players I've liked as just human beings were the fellows who didn't treat me like I was a quickie. There was a lot of fun and laughter. We did silly things.

I was in bed with a player one night when his roommate came in, so we hid under the covers and giggled and tried to pretend that we weren't there. Another time a player came in through the balcony window while a fellow and I were making love. This sort of thing just added to the fun, turned it into good times.

()

My very first player asked me on our very first night for oral sex. I told him I didn't know anything about it, that I'd never done it. And I guess that really shocked him.

None of the fellows ever knew how old I was, because I never told them the truth about my age. Not that I lied, I just never gave them an answer. This first player thought I'd been married only about fifteen years, and he couldn't believe that I'd been married fifteen years and never had any oral sex with my husband.

I said, "That's just something he never thought of or never did." We had just never done it to each other at all.

So when the player asked me to do it for him, I said, "I don't know how to. And I don't even know if I'd enjoy it."

He said, "Would you be willing to try it if I could teach you?"

I said, "Sure, why not?" You know.

So he proceeded to teach me. I didn't like it. Not that it disgusted me. I just didn't get any satisfaction out of it. But my thoughts were, well, if it makes him happy and he's enjoying it, there's no big problem. But I got no sexual pleasure out of it. Not then, and not to this day, and it's tiring to me. I enjoy doing it for some people, because I know it turns them on. And that's fine.

This is always one of the first things an athlete asks you to do. Maybe a married player asks for it because he wants to get a special little extra thrill, or he's afraid of picking up a social disease by having straight sex with another woman. So I guess he figures that if he can get a girl to give him—what do they call it?—a blow job, he can get his satisfaction without worrying what it's going to do at home to his family.

I'm just totally convinced that men get a big, big thrill out of it. But to be truthful, I've yet to figure out exactly why. I guess it just feels awful good to them. I know that when they do it to me, I get an entirely different thrill out of it than with intercourse. I just enjoy it very much. Very much.

Even though almost all of them ask for oral sex, I say no to more of them than not. I tell them that if they don't intend to satisfy me, I won't do it; that I don't get that big a kick out of doing that and nothing else.

They think they can put me on by saying that they'll do it twice: once they'll have a blow job, and then we'll have intercourse. But I've been through enough of those experiences to know that they're not as manly as they think they are. I know they can't do it twice in an evening back-to-back. But a lot of times I'll put *them* on. I'll say, "Okay, I'll give you a blow job."

Then I'll do it a little bit and say, "Oh, I don't feel like it anymore. C'mon. Give me what *I* want." And I usually win out. (Laughs.) I've almost *always* gotten my way. I can get them to such a point of ecstasy that I can pull back and get what I want. By that point, I've got them in the palm of my hand. So to speak. (Laughs.)

I must say that there are two or three fellows that I totally enjoy giving a blow job to, and they don't reach an orgasm either. I like them so much that I would do anything to make them happy. And I definitely get an emotional satisfaction out of this. One fellow was so darned good to me that I'd give him whatever he wanted. And he doesn't always want to have a complete orgasm that way. He just wants you to play with him a little bit that way, and perhaps tease him a little bit. He'll almost always back out himself and ask for the intercourse.

I've found out that the football players who have known me over the years and who have been the closest to me would now much rather come over and just go to bed—without a complete concentration on oral sex.

()

I've never run into any sexually sadistic athletes. I think because they realize they are big and strong that they must just subconsciously work on being extremely gentle, kind and understanding with women. I've never been with one that isn't—if you can use the expression—a *gentleman* in his reactions to treating you as a lady in bed. They are beautiful.

()

A fellow was traded to our team about three years ago, and I had never known him before. One day I happened to be down at the airport saying my goodbyes to our players when they were leaving for an out-of-town game. Evidently, this new fellow noticed me, and I guess some of the other fellows told him about my reputation.

When they came back from that game, the next day in fact, I got a phone call from one of the old players asking me if I'd like to meet the new fellow. This old player was *such* a nice guy—and I'd never been to bed with him, never have yet—that I wasn't bothered by him trying to fix me up. I guess I was a little apprehensive about going cold turkey into a motel room to meet this new fellow. But the old player said, "He's a nice guy. He's the kind of guy who won't push you. If you don't like him, you can just open the door and walk out." So I told him that I'd give it a stab.

I went to the motel room, and when I saw the new fellow I went bananas. He was so gorgeous, and so great. I guess I got to his motel room about eight o'clock at night. Three hours later, we were still talking. I was getting so Goddamned horny just looking at him, I started thinking to myself: for God's sakes, when are we going to do something. He's sitting in a chair, and I'm sitting on the bed all this time. And he wouldn't move.

Finally I thought that maybe if I went to the bathroom, it would move him off that damned chair. That's what I did, and I'll be darned that when I came out of the bathroom he had moved over to the bed. I sat down close to him and kind of pushed myself up next to him. I think I really made the first move, but I did because he was such a nice guy. I really admired this fellow because he really just didn't want to jump on me.

When we finally did make it, I think that was one of the most beautiful sexual affairs I ever had with a player. I must admit: he was married, and he missed his family. He was so lonesome and really so horny that he started to have a climax while I was just playing with him. When I rode home that night, just thinking about what had happened almost brought tears to my eyes. I thought: what a warm guy.

We went together for almost two years. What a beautiful guy. Anytime he came to my place, he could come at two o'clock in the morning and stay for twenty minutes and leave, and I'd never shut the door in his face next time. That's how nice a guy he was.

()

I wish I could figure out a way to stop guys from having early climaxes. Even this fellow I date very steadily now

can't go more than three strokes without coming. I've read—
and I don't know whether it's true or not—that an early
climax is supposed to be a form of guilt. But I think that a lot
of it is willpower. And a lot of it, too, is *man*.

If only a man could put this thing out of his mind and
concentrate on not coming right away. Just like they get
down on that football field and concentrate on blocking
another guy. That's the same thing he's got to do in bed:
concentrate on not having a climax himself until he's
satisfied the woman completely. I think it can be done, but
not being a man I just don't know. (Laughs.)

A lot of times I've had some of these big strong players
apologize for coming too early. They always have excuses:
they were tired, or they'd done it with their wives earlier.
They have all sorts of flimsy excuses.

I've always gotten a kick out of the big, brawny football
player who's going to take me home and make love three or
four times in one evening. I mean, I go home with him
knowing that he's not going to make it past once or twice, if
he's lucky. And I don't say anything when I hear this. I figure
just let him go along with whatever his excuse is.

Some of them will say, "Well, you were just so good, you
took everything out of me, and now I just can't do it
anymore."

Then I say, "That's fine. I enjoyed it so much, who cares?"
But I know as soon as they come home with me that I'm not
going to get three or four times from these guys. They talk
more than they deliver. I've never had one that could do that
yet. Twice, yes. But that's the most.

()

There was a football party one time, and I guess the
fellows decided they wanted to see how many of them could
make it with Millie that might. So while I was in bed with
one, another watched. Then when the first one finished, the

second one came on. There were about five players at the party. I was the only woman, so I guess you could say that in a true sense it was an orgy.

I've only been drunk about four times in my life, but all of us were pretty totalled out on liquor that night. I had no idea when I went to this party that this was going to happen. No idea at all.

After the party got going, somebody said, "Let's have an orgy." So we did. One got off, another got on. All five of them. It probably lasted an hour, hour and a half. I enjoyed them all, had a ball. It was a lot of fun. I was with each of them only once apiece, and there was always an audience of four watching. All in one room.

When I sobered up the next day, I thought I'd been pretty much of a damned fool, really.

Another time I was driving with four players on the expressway. I was keeping rather regular company with one of them at the time. All of a sudden I said to him, "Just for the hell of it, let's not you and me be together tonight. Let's have a great big orgy."

Before you knew it, there were ten or so guys from this one team dropping in and out of this one player's room all night. Honestly, I couldn't even keep count that night. All I know is that every time I turned around, somebody else was coming in the room. That night, I was sober; I'd been drinking, but I was sober.

The way it turned out, that was the beginning of the end of my relationship with that one fellow. He didn't object to my volunteering for the orgy, but it never was the same after that happened. Whenever he would come into town after that, he wouldn't call me for a date. Instead, he would tell me that other players wanted to be with me, or that he was sending certain fellows over to my place. I mean, I felt like I was *really* being used. Like I was a volleyball. I wasn't enjoying it at all.

From what I can remember, I had orgasms with all these fellows at both orgies. Five the first time; however many there were the second time. Nothing stops me from that. Oh, if a guy's been drinking a lot and he really can't do anything, I just get tired of trying and tell him to forget it. I mean, I'm not getting anything out of it. They can get hard when they're drunk, but they can't have a climax. Oh, they think they can; they think that any minute it's going to happen. In the meantime, he's drained everything out of me. I might as well just pick up a newspaper and start reading it. I've become totally bored with the whole thing.

Usually, though, I orgasm instantly. I realize now, looking back, that I'm sure I had this sexual potential in me all my life, but it was just never brought out. I don't know if sometimes now I feel that I'm over-sexed or if I'm just dying for somebody to really love me. I want to find a guy who'll love me just so damned much, and who I'll love so damned much.

I've been watching some of these young players who are married, and they really seem so very, very happy. I feel I can decipher some of these relationships, tell the phoney ones from the real ones. Some of them are going to go a long way—when I see them holding hands and going to the movies together and out to dinner together. You know, having someone to share things with.

I know I want all of that kind of thing. But I want it with someone who'll love me. I feel I have so much love to give to somebody. And maybe I needed these seven years in football to get rid of all these inner frustrations of mine. But I realize now that none of these football affairs were true love.

()

After those orgies, I guess I got a beautiful reputation. You know, like poison.

I went to a party this year and had one of the fellows say, "Okay, I want a blow job. I've heard about your reputation." And two other guys were egging me on to do it to him. So I did. Or I started to. But I didn't finish. I got my way again. I got my intercourse with him, and we stayed together all night. You know us devious women. Terrible, huh?" (Long smile.)

()

I won't ask every player I'm in bed with to go down on me. Only the ones that I feel a very deep warmth for.

Now, I know that I'll go down on a guy if he asks me to—and I don't mean all of them, but just the ones I care about—yet I don't ask a man to go down on me. But that's for the same reason that I can't go knocking on a guy's door some night when *I'm* horny, just like guys knock on my door. They can refuse me, but I can't refuse them. I don't know whether this has to do with them being *males,* or whether it's just me, or whether I should be more forward, or what.

There's one that visits me quite frequently now who'd probably be the only one in my whole life that I'd ever want to marry, and I don't even have to ask him to go down on me. I know he will. I just eagerly look forward to it; I just go absolutely out of my mind.

I know that a man going down on a woman is just one more little part of sex. But a lot of men don't like to do that. I remember asking a guy to do that to me and being turned down. I felt rejected and hurt a little, but I smiled through it all.

I realize that I've been hurt through this whole thing. I've been used, and I've been hurt. But how do I know I haven't hurt them, too? I mean, I know I can only tell about my own feelings. But how do I know what I might have done to some of these guys that are human beings?

I had this incident with a friend of a football player. The man had been married only about nine or ten months, but he came home with me. He could not function sexually, though. He was totally in love with his wife, and he felt guilty about coming to my place, but he wanted to find out what the feeling would be like. And he thanked me. He asked me if I was angry that he was going to leave, and I told him that I wasn't.

I said, "I'm glad you found out that you were really happily married and that you're content with your wife and that you don't need anything else. Now get up and leave. I'm not mad at you at all."

()

It's never mattered to me if a football player I make love with is married. Look, this is what broke up my marriage: a man's extra-curricular activities. I think the one thing I made up my mind about when I got divorced was that I'd never go out with a married man. I told myself I *never* could. I didn't want to hurt anybody the way I was hurt.

Then I got exposed to this world after being sheltered for so long, and I found out that if it wasn't going to be me then it would be someone else who went out with these married guys. All these men want to do is find out whether the grass is greener on the other side. I feel that a man is an animal—a beautiful, beautiful animal. And an animal cannot stick with one female.

I think the reason the married ones come to me is that with me they can find out if the grass is greener without getting hurt. They know I'll keep my mouth shut. Just like now: I'm not giving you any names of any of these players. I'd never hurt them. I haven't hurt a one yet.

I had two close calls, though. But I always keep a little cover-up story in my mind in case there's a problem. One night a fellow was supposed to come over, but he didn't show up after I waited a long time. A couple of nights later I saw him at a bar, and I was too stupid to look past his left shoulder. I walked up to him and said, "Where were you the other night?" And suddenly I saw his wife standing behind him. So really fast I added on: "Where were you when I tried to reach you to invite you to Joe's birthday party?" I mean, there really was going to be a birthday party for Joe. It's lucky I've always got these projected cover-up answers.

Another time I was driving my car around one of the player's houses because I wanted to see if he was home. His wife came out and recognized my car, and I gunned out of there. The player knew that I was there, and he protected us by telling his wife that it wasn't my car.

I'm sure there are several wives who know about me. I mean, I know there are some of them who just don't like me. I can tell by the way they look at me—with misgiving eyes. They've got to know that their husbands cheat. I mean, they've got to.

I knew when it was happening to me. I never confronted my husband with it, but I knew. I think all women realize it when it's happening.

So when a football player's wife looks at me, I know she's thinking: is that the one, or is it the woman sitting next to her, who's been in bed with my husband? Or is it one of her girlfriends?

They have no real proof or evidence. But they know. They do.

()

I was very attracted to athletes when I was in high school. The build of a man was very important to me then, and more so later, but I ended up marrying a man who was short, scrawny and built terrible. I really don't know if my demands for good physiques in a man now is a fetish or hangup of mine or what. Looks to me are very irrelevant, though, basically. I like what's inside the man, what comes from within him.

I never used to give much thought to how a man was hung until after my divorce. But I soon found out that it helps if a man is well-hung. Let me put it to you this way: it has its advantages. Still, some of these big guys aren't as big as some people might think they are. There's always been this story about the biggest man on our football team—big in every way but one. And I know this to be true, because I was with him.

I'd been told about it, so I wasn't that surprised when I saw how small it was. But if I didn't know, I couldn't have believed what I saw. He didn't say anything, but I have had some of them with small ones apologize. Over the years I've learned though, that it's how they use it and not how big it is that counts.

And when I talk about how they use it, it gets back to the question of what is sex. Is it how long it lasts? Is it how tender it is? The few fellows that I've truly enjoyed have really made love to me in bed. I can't describe it in any other way but that. With a few of them, it's really been romance.

There's one player that I see from time to time who often would tell me he'd rather rent a motel room than come over to my apartment. Just for the romanticism of being in a motel room. He and I would take showers together, baths together. We'd make love on the floor, in the bathtub. And it was never uncomfortable in the bathtub. Rather fun, actually.

So what's important to me is whether I'm romanced or whether I'm used. And it's probably a very fine line that separates sex from romance, but I can feel it. Especially when a man takes me in his arms and holds me after the sex is over; he's in no hurry to unclutch me. Then I can look at him and tell him, "Hey, I really think you're a super guy. I really like you."

Once in a situation like that I said to the man, "Would it upset you if I told you I love you?"

He said, "No. It would upset me if you *didn't* tell me you loved me."

This man's stroking while we're making love is just so even and pretty. And if he feels he's going to reach a climax too soon, he just stops. He'll just hold me and talk to me for a few minutes to break the subject of sex. Then when we start going at it again, he looks at me as if to say: "Hey, I really care."

◊

Most of my athletes have been football players. I was in baseball for a while, but not with too many of them.

I used to love baseball, but it got to be such a slow, draggy game that I lost interest in it, and in most of the players, although there are one or two baseball players who come to town that I see every year. They always tell me to call them at the motel, because they say they can't carry my phone number with them. So I do, and leave a message for them at the desk. Then they always call back and keep in touch with me. But there are only those one or two baseball fellows.

It's just that I like the bloody game of football so much. I like the contact. Nobody likes to believe I'm a peace-loving person because I like the contact so much. I love to see a good fight on the football field. It's just the game that attracts me, and not necessarily the size of the players.

I once went out with some hockey players, and that was pretty short-lived. I found them to be the crudest, nastiest bunch of men I was ever out with in my life. They had no tact. I was dancing with one of these hockey fellows one night, and while we were out there on the dance floor, he was poking his finger up my rectum.

Then they invited me to the bar in their hotel. Now I am so used to locker room talk that nobody has to apologize to me for what they say, but the way these guys talked was vulgar, filthy, downright crude. I didn't want to go to bed with any of them, and I started to walk out of the bar.

Two or three of them followed me outside. They really weren't going to let me go. I told them to stop following me or I'd holler for a hotel guard who was nearby. Finally, I made it to my car. Then these jerks took their whiskey glasses and threw them at my car. I've *never* had a football player mistreat me like that.

Oh, I guess there once was a player who wanted to have sex in the rectum with me. But I completely, totally refused. Mainly because when I was a child I had an operation down there, so I'm very sensitive. I did try it once, but it hurt. So no way any more. I mean, even when they give me an enema in the hospital I die a thousand deaths.

But I wanted to try everything once. Once before I die. ◦ Now I feel that I have. If you could have told the woman who won an honorary life membership in the P.T.A. ten years ago that someday she'd have an orgy with professional football players, well, I would have said, "No way. Not me." For seven solid years I really lived, and I enjoyed every moment. I don't know if it's over completely, just that it's less.

I think if I were to tell my ex-husband about the players I've been with—and I never would tell him—he would look me straight in the face and call me a Goddamned liar. He couldn't believe that I have attracted the men I've attracted. Maybe I was trying to prove something both to myself and to my ex-husband, without him knowing it. He just used to think that I was about the worst thing sexually that ever walked the face of this earth.

( )

What really got to me in the last few years—and I've put a stop to it now—is a player showing up in the middle of the night at my place. They'd be out with a young girl and buy them drinks and wine them and dine them. Then they'd get the girl to her front door, and the girl would probably say, "This is it." Then along about two-thirty in the morning there'd be a knock on my door, and they'd come in long enough to get their quickie and then leave.

But I don't let that happen anymore. I figure that if they want me they should talk to me. I'm a human being. I'll give them a drink and talk to them, too. If they want to come to my house, by God, they should stay overnight. I mean, I know this can't be done in every case. Some guys have to go home to their wives.

But generally I'm not going to let myself be used for a fifteen-minute piece of ass. Really.

That did used to happen more times than not. And I always could tell when it would. But I guess I was trying to prove something to myself—that I was worthy of them. I hadn't had good sex for so many years of my life that when I did find something good, I just wanted it. I wanted it any time of the day, night, morning. I wanted it by anybody I thought was attractive.

Hey, it was a big ego trip to be with these big, good-looking guys. I've yet to figure out how God put it all together when he made them intelligent and strong and handsome. I think I was willing to give up anything of myself to be with them. It was the kind of personal satisfaction that I needed. I know they saved me from a lot of sessions on a psychiatrist's couch. I know this.

I know totally that I was on an ego trip. Even with the ones I didn't go to bed with, I formed a friendship. And a friendship is a form of an ego trip, too. I mean, it's nice to be friends with somebody who's a little bit important. Sure, the garbage collector is a nice guy, too, but who knows about him?

I was ready for a complete nervous breakdown by the time I had left my husband. Not out of love; there wasn't an ounce of love left. Just out of the fact that I'd been attached to somebody for twenty-four years—from the time I was a kid. I knew no other world. I went from a home environment with my parents to making a home environment. Suddenly,

41 *millie*

an only-child, spoiled brat like myself—someone who'd never really had it bad, who'd always had it comfortable—was now left to face this great big world all by herself. And I was frightened.

Then when I found myself with all these football players, I felt that, hey, I wasn't as bad as my ex-husband thought I was. I mean, I was attracting these good-looking boys. And it meant something to me. It saved me from having to lay down on a psychiatrist's couch and say, "I'm an inadequate moron."

Thinking that way about things, I was able to handle all the quickies: Oh, maybe the first year I was dumb to what was going on. But it didn't take long to get smart and see what they were after.

Let me say this, though: while they were using me, I was using them. I think they knew that, too. I don't think they could be fooled by this. If they were, I don't think they're as smart as I give them credit for being.

the gert and gladys show

gert... *Thirty-seven years old, short, chunky, moonfaced, loyal. For the past ten years, she has been a secretary for a variety of professional sports organizations throughout the country. She is very good at her work; acutely perceptive. Currently she is the number one girl in the office for a big league team. There was only one man who ever satisfied her. Not an athlete. He married someone else, but when he comes to town on business he calls Gert. And she sees him. She has never married.*

gladys... *Thirty-two years old, a bit taller, thinner, bustier and more sentimental than her good friend Gert. She was married to a gentleman she describes as "a non-traveling man." Before the divorce, they had a son, five-years-old now. Gladys has been a desk clerk for a half dozen years at a hotel used by many teams from all major pro sports. She, too, does nice work.*

Both speak huskily, laugh often, kid themselves and each other. They agreed to a joint interview in their Midwest city. The three of us had Scotch, spare ribs, spaghetti, cole slaw and a great amount of an okay Cabernet. Hell of an evening.

GLADYS: I put the women who come in contact with athletes into three categories. There are the innocent, the knowledgeable, and the I-don't-give-a-shit. That's what I call them—the knowing ones like Gert and me, and the ones out to prove they're women. The young ones I feel sorry for. I really do. They don't know what they're getting themselves

43

in for. They are enamored of the athlete, with his image and his importance. They think that the greatest thing going is to be with this person, and that whatever the guy says is good. And then they're going to get hooked into going to bed with the guy. The young girl is just impressed.

GERT: I don't give any thought to the behavior of the older ones, the ones Gladys says don't give a shit. I figure they know what in the hell they're doing. They're just seeking relief.

GLADYS: If some of these girls who mess with athletes have a conscience, it must bother them. It's got to. They must know that they're not the only one this guy screws. But Gert and I have a conscience. We can't accept this business of just going to bed with anyone.

GERT: Aw, some of those older broads are just horny. Gotta be.

GLADYS: I can't say if it's only horniness, or ego, or insecurity. All I know is that with me it's a sense of values and morals and respect. I have no goddamn, friggin' ego. I'm not gorgeous. I'm not shapely. Just that I would rather go without screwing fifty thousand guys a year then to have one guy say that I was a tramp. It's important to me to have this respect with all the athletes who come to our hotel. I don't care to sleep with any of those guys. I don't give a shit if it's Bobby Orr or Jerry West. All that's important to me is doing my best for them on the job and gaining their friendship—without having to date them.

GERT: That's it. The job is important to us. Sure, we're human. We get horny. But I realize that I can't mess with the guys in my sport because I'm known. However...when I look at some of the sexy guys in other sports, I think: now if I gave them a phony name (bawdy laughter) and just disappeared into the night, nobody would know.

GLADYS: Listen, I could just go to sleep with somebody and just be held by them without any sex happening, and that would be all right too. I love to be cuddled by somebody, to feel wanted and warm and cared for. I don't want to be made to feel like I'm a friggin' machine.

GERT: And most of the athletes look upon most women as machines.
GLADYS: Definitely.

()

GLADYS: Sometimes I've been asked by an athlete who's staying at our hotel to fix him up with a girl. I say, "Look, you're over twenty-one, right? Find your own." That's one of my classic answers. Or, a non-classic answer is: "Screw you." I mean, what's wrong with *me*, honey? (Laughs.)
GERT: I tell my players: "I've got better things to do with my time than run around with girls. If you want some names of some very nice men I know, I'll be glad to give *them* to you."
GLADYS: The athlete kind of looks on your girlfriends with different eyes than you do.

()

GERT: The first team I worked for had these dark, dingy offices way out in the boondocks. It was my first week there and I was all alone in the office because everybody was at practice. All of a sudden this one player walks in, a good-looking guy. He starts talking to me and walking around my desk, you know. He puts his hands on my shoulders and he's giving me a little shoulder rub. I am just petrified. Absolutely petrified. I didn't know what was expected of me. I didn't know what he was going to do, and I just stiffened up. I answered his questions very curtly, and I think he realized right then and there that he was scaring me. So he backed off and left—for which I will always be thankful. I found out later that apparently he was sort of a scout for the other players. He was going to find out what was up with the new secretary. The guy was a sex scout. After that day, I was never really bothered by another player.

GLADYS: When I first came to work at the hotel, I just drooled when I saw some of these athletes. Like Gert, I was thinner in those days, too. But when they asked me out, I knew they had only one reason. I was there. I was convenient. They didn't have to go out looking for it. In the early days a lot of them would come up to me and say, "Hey, why don't we go out?" And I'd say, "Where? To my mother's house?" That'd scare them off. I had a football player call me at the desk one time and ask me to come to his room. I told him I was sorry, but that was against the rules. He said, "Bullshit on the rules," I told him, "Not bullshit. Those are my rules, too. My moral rules. I work here, and this is the place of my security and virginity." He hung up on me. But lately if an athlete asks me out, I know he's at his last resort. (Laughs.) Like now, when I see all these other broads at the sports bars—these super-shapely and busty and thin girls—I know where I stand. So does Gert. Maybe that's why we stay together: so we don't have to worry. It keeps us safer.

()

GERT: Girls do most of the picking up at the sports bars. They go up to an athlete and talk about that night's game, or ask for an autograph. The girls know who they're talking to. It's all planned out. I see it all the time at this one bar.

GLADYS: You know, there's a mother-daughter combination at this bar.

GERT: It's unbelievable. Makes me sick to my stomach to talk about it.

GLADYS: What happens is that the mother usually entices the players.

GERT: Her daughter is very attractive. But I've seldom seen the daughter talk. She just sits there, the daughter. She's got beautiful, bleached-blonde hair. By the time the players get there, the mother has her all propped up at a good seat at the bar.

GLADYS: I think they leave the game early just to get good seats.

GERT: Right. And the daughter just sits there. Never says boo. And the players keep walking around and around the bar.

GLADYS: Then the mother gets very forward. She's definitely the promoter. The mother's not very attractive but she is well-preserved. Nice looking, I guess. She starts the conversations with the guys. And they are really intrigued.

GERT: You can see the players start flocking around the daughter after she's introduced by the mother. I'm sitting at the other end of the bar, watching all this going on. The players are standing around the daughter, but the *spillover* is going to the mother. She's using the daughter as bait. I don't think it's that she's pitching her so much. Just using her as bait. And I don't think she tells players right away that this girl is her daughter. I saw them for a whole season before I knew it. The mother does not like to broadcast this.

()

GLADYS: Athletes get sex thrown at them all the time. And if they're on the road for more than a couple of days, they tell themselves they're horny. And they don't give a shit particularly who it is or what it is. They just want their two minutes of satisfaction.

GERT: And most of the time it doesn't cost them anything. But they've got human desires. I don't blame them.

GLADYS: Well, you can't condemn them, but sometimes I wonder. For two years I knew this relief pitcher on a just-friends basis. I mean, just kidding around. Nice friendship stuff. But then he comes to see me one day last year and says, "C'mon, Gladys. You know what it's like." He was sober, too. I say, "I beg your pardon. *What* are you talking about?" And he says, "You and I could...." I says, "We could what? No sir. We could never." I was crushed that he'd made me an offer. All of a sudden I was put way down. And it was just because he's had it easy with other girls. But when his wife's in town with him, I'm treated different.

GERT: All athletes use the same lines with a girl. It's always implied that they're a professional athlete, a star with such and such a team. And when there's a turndown, they're insulted. Like: what do you *mean* you won't go to bed with me. What's the *matter* with you? Some will pout, some will get mad, others will be really crushed because you're puncturing their egos. They try to put *you* on the defensive. Like, you are really at fault. As far as they're concerned, they're just tops; they cannot understand somebody not wanting to screw them. In every single town, girls are thrown at them. But I wouldn't touch any of them with a ten-foot oar.

GLADYS: You see, when you know what's expected of you before you even get started on a date, all the challenge and mystery and speculation is *gone.* And that takes a lot out of a woman. But athletes do have class about them.

GERT: And confidence, too. When I was working in professional golf, I once got picked up by a golfer with a Lincoln Continental and his nameplate on the dashboard. You think I wasn't impressed? But I also have this Midwest upbringing and there's no way I can lose it. I never went to bed with any of them. And there's another thing: I will never go out with a married man if I know he's married. If I don't know and happen to wind up with a married guy, then it's unfortunate.

GLADYS: It's your own damn fault. (Laughs.)

()

GLADYS: My babysitter asked me to take her nineteen-year-old sister to a hockey game one night, and I said sure, fine. I didn't know this young girl was nothing less than wild.

Before the evening was over—we went to a bar in a large group after the game—this girl and I end up with two married players from the visiting club. The four of us went to some joint in the suburbs where I had an ex-sister-in-law who danced topless, then we had breakfast at another place. By then I was ready to take the players back to the hotel. But the girl wasn't ready to end the evening. She wanted to take the guys back to my house, so we did. I figure we'll just have a cup of coffee or a drink or something, and *then* I'll take them back to the hotel. But in the meantime, she takes this one guy into my bedroom. The other player and I just sat in the living room, and all of a sudden, I guess out of some sense of ego, he tried to put the make on me. These other two are in the bed having a great time, and we're out there hearing it all. It was adorable, really. You better believe I was embarrassed. Mortified. This had never happened to me before. My house is so small you sit in the living room and hear everything going on in the bedroom. Even with the door closed. The guy with me is listening and trying to get less horny. But he kept getting more horny, and I kept getting more embarrassed. I took him in the kitchen to give him a cup of coffee, but he tries to kiss me. So I push him away. I said to him, "Look, before this night ever got started, you knew I knew you were married, and that took care of that right there. Secondly, you're an athlete and because of my job you know I don't mess with athletes. I'm sorry for what's going on in the bedroom, but I didn't plan it." I told him I couldn't perform. So for a couple of years I was called a dud. Miss Dud.

GERT: The guys on this one club had a party to celebrate the end of a season. It was supposed to be a stag party, but they all pooled their pennies and hired a pro. Imagine, one pro for fifteen or seventeen guys. And she is making the rounds. They must have paid her a fortune, because she was really *working*. She had one in the bedroom while the others stood in line outside the bedroom door. My gosh, she must have killed herself. I don't know how the hell she could do it.

I understand there were a few guys at the party who just watched. All the watchers were married, but not all the married guys just watched. They did have themselves a party, and when I heard about it my only reaction was: typical.

()

GERT: Not all the men in sports are the same, you know. There's such a thing as public relations directors and traveling secretaries who come on the road with a team, and as far as Gladys and I are concerned these guys are a little bit different than the players. They are management, so they have to be much more discreet. Just like Gladys and I do. They don't try to compete with the players as far as, like: I am male and I am supreme. And so they put women on a different level. These guys are mostly a little bit upper class. So we look at them differently. I'm talking about PR guys, traveling secretaries, managers, coaches, trainers— management guys. So I have associated myself with, uh, hah, two trainers, one PR director (pauses to giggle with Gladys)...one hockey trainer I have known for eight years who's a dirty ole man. (Gladys continues to laugh.) That SOB has gone around and around with me for I don't know how long. And I've always said, "No way, you mother." We're really good friends. We respect each other, but...it's always been a battle. And I always won until once I didn't win. And then I thought, aw shit, what in the hell did I do that for? Then there was this PR director from one of the hockey leagues that came on too strong.
GLADYS: Which one you talking about? The same as mine?
GERT: Well, there's only one PR director we're talking about. Right?
GLADYS: This team here or somebody else's?

GERT: We gotta be talking about the same one. Who else? That tall, beady-eyed bastard. (Both howl.)

GLADYS: The guy is really super. Right Gert?

GERT: He is really.

GLADYS: And he has accepted both situations gloriously.

QUESTIONER: What do you mean, both situations?

GLADYS: Hers and mine. (Laughs, as then does Gert.)

GERT: We have never even discussed this before. It's coming out. Comparing notes. Right now.

GLADYS: But you know something? The reason why I've sensed it is that he has the same respect and admiration for both of us. Even after.

GERT: Yah, he's good people.

GLADYS: And he's a bachelor. So there were no strings attached.

GERT: Yep. He's a bachelor.

GLADYS: So we both have the same fondness for the same guy. Even after and during and before, without even knowing it.

GERT: Right. He's good people. He really is. But I tell you what turned me off. The night he picked up a black girl in a bar while I was sitting there. I don't know what happened.

GLADYS: That would have turned me off, too, if I had known it.

GERT: I don't think I really had too much to do with him after that.

GLADYS: It ended for me four or five years ago.

GERT: He's still around.

GLADYS: Super guy. He really is.

GLADYS: He still adores us. He has shown no partiality. And he wouldn't hold it against either one of us. He still thinks the world of us. As people.

GERT: Knowing he was an interlude to us.

GLADYS: He was one person who classified us like we are. In other words, we're not pushovers, easy makes, all-team types, all-player types.

GERT: We go for the person.

GLADYS: That's right. There's a depth in there in us that somebody has got to see.

GERT: Your relationship with him goes back before mine. I feel definitely that the man was not playing both of us at the same time.

GLADYS: No, I'm sure he was not. He really is not that kind of person at all.

GERT: No, he isn't. He's really very sensitive.

GLADYS: He's not totally a playboy because he is sensitive. And people that have emotions that are deep—like ours—you do not play with. And I feel very fine about discovering what we both did, Gert and I. Because we're two of a kind. And I feel that if he values one of the other the same, then he's got two Goddamn good broads that he's experienced.

GERT: I feel exactly the same. I very much like and respect Gladys. I feel our values are the same way. Which means we found something in a person to like and enjoy.

GLADYS: Regardless of whatever happened, he's never, never made me feel any different than when I was sleeping with him five years ago. Next time I see him, I won't humiliate him and tell him, "Hey, I hear you slept with Gert." No way. Because I respect both of them. And her even more.

the white chickee

tina... *twenty-five, five feet six inches tall, one hundred twenty-seven pounds, sharp-featured, large, quickly darting dark eyes often filled with humor. Telephone company craftswoman full-time, club singer sometime. Has been described in sports literature as "a girl who can give a thoroughly professional scouting report on every team in the National Basketball Association." Says she has been involved sexually with three black superstars of the NBA and dated several other black superstars "by design. I won't go out with anybody, any black, who is not a name, because the chance of us being accepted in public is greater than if I was with a black nobody." She is white. Father was "an old country Italian"; mother "an unbelievable bigot from Kansas." Hospitalized after a nervous breakdown at twenty-one, then saw a psychiatrist. Diagnosis attributed emotional problems—and dating of tall blacks—to attempted rape by her five-foot eleven-inch stepfather when she was twelve-years-old. Psychiatrist told her she sought men "totally opposite to my stepfather." Tall men make her feel "very, very protected."*

One of them, for eight months in 1967 and early 1968, was seven-foot Wilt Chamberlain, one of the most significant figures in the history of American basketball. Describes him as "the heartthrob of my life." During their affair, she wrote an erotic poem that "makes 'The Love Book' look like 'Mary Poppins'."

Excerpts from Tina's poem to Wilt Chamberlain:

The KING & i

a BODY, big and black and fine
strong, but gentle and very kind
the BODY i want to be all mine
the most WONDERFUL i'll ever find.

he fits INSIDE me as no other has
if not with he, with no one will i ever see a bed
HOW does one let a peasant pass
where a KING has tread?

the touch of him excites me
my blood begins to boil inside
HE is the best there will ever be
it didn't take me long to decide.

I had a good friend at the box office, so for the playoffs, I was given a very good seat directly on courtside. That was the year that Wilt and the Philadelphia 76ers won the title, and during that series he damn near ended up in my lap. I caught him eyeing me a couple of times. I knew that he noticed me, and I found him very attractive. So after that series I just sent him a letter and congratulated him and told him I was glad that he had finally won his championship, et cetera et cetera; I never expected to hear any more about it. And about two months later my phone rings about four one morning. He said it was Wilt and he was calling from New York. At four in the morning? I said sure, right, and slammed down the phone. So the phone rang again right away and he said it really was Wilt and that he had my letter and would I like him to read it right now. We rapped for over an hour, and he was really charming. He said he was coming to town in a couple of days and could I see him.

As it was I was on vacation, so I thought we could arrange to get together. It was like, you know, a dream come true to meet your idol.

I came to meet basketball players because my sister worked in an auto agency with one. For a while I dated a white player, then I kind of got to know Nate Thurmond of the Golden State Warriors. Nate is a gentleman; he is very civilized. He never discusses women with another man. He's a kind, kind, gentle man who loves people and never wants to hurt anybody. Wilt intimated to me that he had spoken to Nate about me earlier and that Nate had said we were friends but that was all. Later, Nate told me that he told Wilt he might not go over too well with me. All Nate knew then was that I talked to black players but not what else I might do. So Wilt didn't have any reason to expect anything—despite his tremendous ego. Wilt has an ego that won't quit.

Before he came over that first night we had a couple more telephone conversations, probably about eight hours altogether. I'd never said anything in my letter about going to bed. But he did ask once on the phone if I were sexually active or not. I told him I felt that at this point in time it wasn't any of his damn business. And he said, "Well, people hear things and people talk." And I said, "People lie, too." I wasn't giving him any bait of any kind. I figured if he wanted to come over to see me, what happened would happen. If not, not. And that was the way it went. But I wasn't going to bait him in any way; I wasn't going to make any promises I might not want to keep.

When he walked in the door of my apartment I just about came uncaged. He was just so terribly attractive to me. It was like the whole world came right in place. It was the type of thing like, well, like some girls would react to a Paul Newman. Wilt really did it for me. Everything fell together. I'd had my eye on him for five years, so (laughs) you know. ...He is a handsome man, very handsome. Just everything about him is handsome. He moves with a grace that a man that size shouldn't have. He dresses with a flair unique to him. I have never seen an athlete who can carry it off quite as well as Wilt. Unique is the only word I can use to describe this man. And selfish, unfortunately. But unique.

It was a funny thing that first night. My hair was really in an atrocious mess, so I had put on a blonde wig. Wilt knew I had red hair from our phone conversations, so I don't think he thought he was in the right place at first. But I convinced him, so he sat down and had a drink. We talked and watched TV maybe two, three hours. I was sober; I don't drink. We just talked and sort of got acquainted. Then he picked me up and carried me into the bedroom. I'd never had any fantasies about going to bed with Wilt. When I looked at him, strangely enough I didn't look at him sexually—just the beautiful specimen that he was. But I think that he had made up his mind he was going to get me one way or another that first night, because that was the demeanor about him when he came in: I'm here, you're lucky, appreciate me while you can. But, very honestly, when he picked me up in his arms I didn't resist him at all. I wanted to be very close to him.

I was only nineteen at that time, but I'd had some experience with sex already. A bit. (Laughs.) But Wilt was the first black man I'd ever been to bed with. And, like, that's sort of starting at the top. (Laughs.) If you know what I mean. He's obviously a big man. Built proportionately. He was hung better than any man I'd ever seen before. Before, yes. Since, no. (Laughs.) And that made him mad, too, when I told him later. But when I lose my temper, I lose my temper. Wilt has a gentleness about him with handling a woman that I've never come across since, though. And it's funny, no matter what you know you are to him, no matter how you feel about being in that situation—that you are probably just another piece for him—when you are having sexual relations with him you have the world at your feet. That's the only time he's not selfish. He does everything he can to make you happy, which is a trait you don't find in a lot of men. He was very gentle with me. I mean obviously I wanted him, and I was aggressive. But I was a little apprehensive and a little scared too, I guess. I mean, that was a big dude.

I enjoy sex as long as I feel I am giving. A lot of times I don't feel that I'm being given to, but if I can really say I'm giving out a strong feeling of affection or love or whatever it might be, then I enjoy it very much. I am extremely highly sexed. I thought for a time that I was a nymphomaniac, then I found out there are none, there are just different levels of need. My psychiatrist explained I had a high level but that there was nothing wrong with that. It's a funny thing, though—I can go for months at a time and not have a man. I mean, if the man I want is there, I'll wear him to a frazzle. But if I don't have it, I don't miss it. It's hard to explain, but when you're single you condition yourself to not having a sex life. It's like the time I was going with this married basketball guy. A black superstar. He came to town three times a year. I had this thing with him for three years, and I didn't see another man for sex. So that's nine nights in three years I had a man with me.

I don't think I've been sexually spoiled either by having these large men. It's not the tool, it's what you make of it. You know, like some guys are really, really put together. And they're really selfish bastards. They're in and out and then it's over. Yet you take the not-so-well-built man and he will compensate for what he feels he lacks and will do more for you and try to please you.

With Wilt, it was I think the first time I had completely loved a man. I picked a real loser, but I did love him. Since him I have had some better orgasms but as you grow older I think your feelings grow more intense. They're based on different values than when you're nineteen. But Wilt made me realize what it means to really love somebody; how much it means you have to give up of yourself. And a lot of times, all the crap you have to take because you love someone. Having him away and things like that. He always used to tell me how much he appreciated me sexually—over the telephone when he was thousands of miles away. I didn't believe too much. But I think he really did appreciate me. In our sex, we shared equally. I don't have any hangups. I don't feel that I'm at all inhibited, and he didn't teach me anything new. He was happy just the way I was. I never told Wilt that I loved him. I wouldn't give him the satisfaction. I knew what I felt. I'd tell him that I loved his body. He thought he had me trapped, but he didn't. I can't really say I'm over him, obviously, because if I was I wouldn't be bitter. But he made me super-hostile a lot of times with some of the things he did.

Like he'd make dates whenever his team came into town. And he'd keep me waiting in the hotel lobby for three or four hours at a time because he wasn't in his room. So one day a bunch of the guys on the 76ers came to the lobby and said, "Hey, you don't have to sit down here. Come up and visit with us in our room until he gets here." They were in a room right across the hall from Wilt. So I put a note on his door and told him where I was and went in and played cards with the guys—Billy Cunningham, Matt Goukas, just a bunch of the guys. And I had a good old time. They were really a great bunch. My back was to the door, and all of a sudden the conversation in the card game just stopped dead. I looked up and Wilt was *glowering* in the doorway. And Cunningham says to him, "Hey, man, the lady was waiting for you four hours. We invited her up, so if you're going to yell, yell at us." Wilt didn't say anything. He just took me by the arm and across the hall. When I got inside his room, I got read the riot act. It was nobody's business, he said, who he slept with. He said he didn't want me socializing with his teammates. I explained to him that if he only had the courtesy to get there at the appointed time, there would have been no need for anyone else to keep me company. We really used to fight. I mean, not physically beat up fights, but verbally harangue each other. And I have an evil mouth. I mean I'm a banshee at times. At least I'm honest about it. When I get mad I go. And I got called everything from honky to soda cracker. I don't even remember all the stuff I called him. But he hurts, he really hurts.

Most of the time I saw him only at my place when his club was in town. We rarely went out anyplace. He really never took me out. I never asked him why but I figured it was because he was ashamed of me. I don't know why I thought that, but I put up with it. I was in love with the man. In the beginning, I'd do anything he asked me. Anything. But then I got to a point where I realized he was playing with me. Although I didn't want to break the relationship off, I just didn't let him push as hard. I remember distinctly one evening he came over and the second half of the movie "The Great Escape" was on TV. We had watched the first half the night before, and he stayed over. So this second night he sashays in around eleven o'clock and says he's ready to go to bed. Well, the movie still had an hour to go, and I was diggin' it. I mean, I was busy. He says, "Hey, baby, don't play with me." I says, "Look, I'm watching a movie. If you want to wait until it's over, fine. If not, there's the door." He got up and left. And I've never been one to like movies, but I got to a point where I wouldn't let him push me. If I didn't like something he was doing, I'd tell him. "I'm not doing it. I don't dig it."

Wilt and I had a great big hairy old fight in February of that next year, 1968, when I turned twenty. He had always teased me and told me he only liked teenagers and after I turned twenty he wouldn't see me anymore. That was a Leap Year, because I remember I called him on February twenty-ninth. He was in Boston. I hunted him down. I called Philly, got hold of his roommate, then called three or four hotels in Boston and finally found him. He was annoyed that I'd been able to reach him because he had wanted to be incommunicado. And I said, "Hey, I haven't heard from you in over a month so I wanted to know where in the hell you were." We got into a big discussion: he had heard that I went to a party with this star from the Cincinnati Royals. That was a completely casual thing. A friend of mine knew this Royal and said he didn't have a date and would I go to the party with him. I said sure, I'd be glad to go as long as the guy, who was married, didn't expect any goodies. You know: I'll go to the party but I want to go home alone. And my friend said that was fine. So we went to the party, and I had a helluva good time. I'm not sure what Wilt heard later, but the NBA has a grapevine that's unbelievable. Wilt told me that since everybody else was screwing around in his backyard, he was gonna move; he was gonna get out of the backyard. He just really came uncaged. But there were no goodies between me and this Royal. I mean, I had what I needed at the time in Wilt. I just didn't need anybody else. But Wilt was all irate and upset and his ego was hurt, and he said he couldn't have all the guys around the league sneering when they saw me with him because I'd done this, he said, and I'd done that. The accusations were absolutely wild. Then I lost my temper. I got vulgar—told him sort of to fly away in another vein. That ended it.

I didn't hear from him again until just a few months ago. He had seen me at a game, and of course I was dressed to kill. I mean, honest. I'm out in my pimpin' clothes when he comes to town because I can't let him know that I'm not having a wonderful time. I have to be lovely. So at the games, he'd look. And if I'd look up at him, he'd look away. He didn't want to get caught. He was playing games. Anyway, there were these two chickees who had the seats next to me. I didn't know either of them, but a lot of times you'll make comments to people sitting alongside of you when you're at a sporting event. I'd got to talking to these two girls—very surfacey. And I guess Wilt saw us talking, because when he called a few months ago he wanted me to introduce him to one of them. I told him I didn't know them. He said, "Well, you can get acquainted." I said, "Look, if you think I'm gonna bust my fanny to do your pimpin', you're crazy. If you want to meet her, you got long legs. At the next game, just step right over that bench, say 'My name is Wilt, how do you do'." He said, "Baby, that ain't cool." I said, "Well, that's the breaks. I am not your dating service. You've done well enough without me for the last few years. You haven't talked to me, haven't bothered me. You've left me completely alone, and I wish you'd continue the practice." He hung up.

I've heard all about this million dollar sex pad house he has now. If it makes him happy, fine. He has a little more difficulty satisfying himself than other men because he's accomplished so much. He really doesn't have anything left to strive for. He has everything. And I think one reason he will probably never marry is because he's afraid: he's afraid to give of himself. There's a lot of women who I'm sure have loved him as much as I loved him. Not his money or his position, just the person that he was. And he can be extremely lovable. But I think he's frightened. He's an extremely defensive man, and the prima donna act he puts on is a big facade. I think he's afraid of being taken advantage of, or hurt, or abused. You know, he grew up and he was always baited and always mocked. Although his height made him what he is, he still resents it a little bit. I think, because it has caused him a lot of pain. I don't think he's capable of loving. Just himself. I don't think he can ever change, not at about thirty-six years old. There are degrees of selfishness, and he is at the ultimate degree. There is no turning back when you get there, when you don't care how badly you damage other human beings for your own self-satisfaction. I don't think anybody ever looks back when they get to that point. Well, they say experience is the best teacher, so maybe somebody else will make out better with him than I did.

O

My real father was typical Italian. He died when I was six. He liked ladies and had a vile temper. But I can honestly say that his sun rose and set on me. I couldn't do a thing wrong. Like, my mother was never allowed to discipline me—and I could get away with murder. I was really a spoiled brat. Now, I spoil myself. I buy myself things that I want. I have what I want when I want it. I don't want to get married and have

children. I like my freedom too much. I don't want to belong
to anybody; I don't want anybody to have papers on me.
Anything I have that I want to be mine I won't share with
somebody else. I like being alone. I read extensively: I love
poetry. And those are means of communication. I do
communicate, but not necessarily with other people.

My mother got an idea from an item in a newspaper
column that I was going out with Wilt. She called me a
nigger lover. She got super-hostile. She told me she would
disown me and that she wouldn't have a daughter. You
know, on and on and on. I told her that if she really felt that
way, she just had to do what she felt and I would do what I
felt. When she saw I wasn't going to back down, that she
wasn't scaring me, she shut up and never said anything more
about it. Now, anytime I date a guy and mention that I like
him, she asks, "Is he black?" That's her first question.

The reaction when I'm out with blacks comes mostly from
Caucasians. The blacks understand. These players were their
brothers who had attained something and therefore had a
right to do what they wanted with whomever they wanted.
But a lot of whites seem to think: "Hey, look at that big
nigger. He must think he's hot stuff with that little white
chickee." I'd hear these kind of comments behind my back.
People would say them loudly enough so that they could be
heard by us—but never that loudly so you'd actually take
offense and have to say something back at them. The only
black player who ever got super-aggravated at this kind of
comment was this married guy I mentioned—the three-
nights-a-year man. He just took his coat in one arm and me
in the other, and we just walked out of the place. When we
got outside, I saw that his fists were clenched and his teeth
gritted and the veins of his neck sticking out. I knew that if
we had stayed in that place a moment longer, there would
have been a helluva brawl or something of that nature. But
those comments never bothered me. I was always
comfortable. I felt that the people who were doing the
commenting were the ones with the problem, not me. This

might sound trite, but I was able to examine individuals and like individuals and they just happened to be black. People weren't looking at me anyway. They looked at who I was with. I was like a fixture, no different than an earring on a woman. You don't notice just earrings, you notice a woman in her entirety.

Black players date almost exclusively white gals. It's a matter of ego. Status symbols. They can have their black wives at home or their black girlfriends almost anytime they want them. But when you come into a strange town, it's nice to take out something a little different. But I haven't seen white players dating black gals. I really don't know why. See, I'm not in anything real tight with any of the white players. The white wives in particular have always shunned me. At player parties, I'm always with the black wives. A couple are very close friends of mine. They know I date black players, and to them I'm just a person. They either like me or they don't as a person. I've been very lucky, because they've been extremely kind to me. One of them asked me once about the black players dating white gals, about what her husband might be doing on the road. She said, "Keep an ear out, and if there's anything curious lay something on him so that he knows I'm hep to it." I guess I'm kind of a go-between. Which is kind of good. I can approach a guy and say, "Hey, you've got a wonderful wife and beautiful kids. Don't blow it. She thinks you're messing." And if the guy were intelligent enough, he'd cool it.

I would say that most of the players in the NBA, white and black, mess around. And that doesn't surprise me at all. If a woman marries a professional athlete, she has to accept it. Pro athletes have women put in front of them on silver platters. They have everything from a Saint Bernard to a French poodle. You know. I mean, every walk of life, every kind of looking woman, anything they want. They can have it, and they know it. And I know it myself. I *never* expected anything from any of the guys. I was tickled just to get a card or a little message from my three-nights-a-year married player; something that showed he knew I was around. But I never expected any gifts or anything of that nature. And, you know, I could have gone to bed with almost any NBA player I wanted. I am a fairly attractive girl. When I want to dress, I dress to kill. I have a really extensive wardrobe. You know, feathers and furs. I have a very basic insecurity; by dressing to kill I feel people are more likely to know I'm there. I want people to know I'm there. I think I would have made a great prostitute if I'd decided to go into the business. I could have made a good living. One player told me once, "Do you know there's guys who go into a town and pay a lot of dough just for an evening on the town with a chick? You know, if you were a call girl you could pull in three hundred fifty dollars a night." I thought about it when I was twenty-one and my job was really dreary. I thought it might be glamorous. But to me sex is a personal thing. It's to be shared with someone you care for and not just everybody.

on the floor

claudia... *thirty years old; black and beautiful... a model and actress; twice divorced; mother of four... a loner as a child in the Southwest; her father was in the Army and didn't live with the family until Claudia was seven-years-old... says that as a child she didn't trust people: "they'd tear up my dolls"... married first time at sixteen, had three children in three years; remarried at twenty-five... says that both husbands were "insanely jealous, with no reason to be"... never been a sports fan but did have one involvement with a National Football League superstar, an unmarried black man with a checkered romantic reputation... their relationship didn't figure, says Claudia, because "my father used to fight physically with my mother, and I don't like violent type men. One lick, and I'm gone." Still sees the football player, whom she calls Billy, but his career is over and things are not the same....*

I had heard that Billy didn't particularly care for black women. As far as I know, there was only one other black woman besides me who has been involved with him. I knew of some of his white women—not that I knew any of them personally. But there were times that I would telephone him, and the party that would answer would be a white woman.

One of the times I called him, and it was during a period we were spending a lot of time together, I got quite upset. This white woman had answered the phone at his apartment, and he told me that she was his maid. You know. So the first time that happened I accepted it, but then she answered on several other occasions, especially late at night. And I asked him what hours his maid had. He finally told me that she was his lady, rather *one* of his ladies. He said not to worry about it, that it was still all right for me to call. But I didn't feel that was exactly right, because I had been intimately involved with him. At that point I told him, "When you fire your maid, call me." That was when we pretty much broke up.

I would ask him why he was attracted to white women. I told him that I wasn't going to play second fiddle to any white woman, or actually to any other woman period. I mean, I had become pretty involved with him, but now he didn't seem to be as interested in me as I was in him. The table changed a little bit, you know.

Billy just came right out and said to me he thought that white women were better to him than black women, that they understood him better. He said, "Now look, Claudia, if you had answered the phone when another woman called, would you have let me talk?" I told him that I would have. I might have pressed him to find out what chick was calling him, but I would have let him talk to her.

He said that the white women were good to him, that one of them was giving him money, that she was doing things for him that I could not or would not do. I thought that a man of his status should be quite capable of taking care of himself—whomever he was with. But then when he said this woman was giving him money. I just thought he must be a weak man. He just seemed to prefer women doing this for him, and that gave me a different outlook toward Billy. Actually, that's when I started pulling away from him.

From what he told me, it seemed that the white women treated him more like a king than I did. He said they'd go along with more things, they were always at his beck and call. I guess the white women he fooled around with were wealthy or had money coming in, and this was something I couldn't give him. If he expected me to give him something just for the privilege of being with him, he could forget it. But still, this was the come on he gave me.

He had even given this one white woman a key to his apartment. I didn't have one; don't even know if I would have accepted one from him. Oh, if our thing had gotten tight enough, possibly I might have taken a key. Possibly. But the way things were, it was like this white woman lived there, as if she were his lady. He wanted me to be his woman, too, but it was like he wanted to slip around, you know, and still hang on to this piece of black meat on the side. Openly he had the white woman, and apparently I was just something extra.

Yet, knowing him like I did, I thought he was very prejudiced against whites. And I thought then that maybe he wasn't telling me the truth about keeping her around for her money. Here, really, is my opinion: he's from the Deep South, and there are a lot of guys like him who suddenly find themselves in a position to get whatever they want; all at once new things are available to them—new people in a new part of the country. He'd been exposed to black women all his life, so a black woman was no big thing to Billy. And he found it exciting that a white woman was now available, that she was *there* for him; almost like a man having a change of life.

I have found that most black men who reach a special category in life tend to want to get involved some way with the white race. You know: they want white women. I can't explain it completely, but it happens. I mean, I have even seen these guys with some white women who can't come close to touching some black women in terms of looks. And these guys are in a position to have almost any black woman they might want. But no. They had to have *this* white woman—thinking maybe they'd look more important if they were seen with her.

I've had some black guys tell me they prefer white women because these women are easier...softer. They said the white women do things I wouldn't even *think* about doing. Things like a tongue bath; you know, being licked from toe to head. Like, whatever the guy wanted the women to do was just fine with her. But there are some morals that you have to have, boundaries that nobody should step over regardless. And I wouldn't do some of those things with a man.

I don't honestly think that these white women who went out with Billy were really in love with him. I don't think they were concerned about him or had any deep feelings for him. Oh, maybe one of them did. She was an older woman with money, and I guess she cared about him because she stuck with him even after he was no longer a big star. But maybe if you're older and you have money, you go for a younger man. That may have been her bag. But all those other white women were there only as long as Billy was a star, and not any longer.

A man's title or status or celebrity value doesn't excite me. I don't care if you walked up and told me you were the Secretary of the Treasury. It wouldn't matter to me—unless maybe you were in a position to print me some money. (Laughs.) But really, a man's position alone wouldn't move me. He has to appeal to me on other levels.

()

I went out with a white man only once. He seemed to be nervous in my company, and we never went out again. In fact, he was the only white man I ever dated. Just that once, too.

I'm not saying that white men turn me off, just that no white man I ever felt like being with has ever approached me. If you get ten approaches, nine of them normally are black. And usually the one white who approaches you doesn't come on right. It's not that you reject him because he's white, but he's just hesitant about approaching you in the first place. And, you know, if nine black men come up to you, normally you'll find one of them who is cool.

I don't have any objections to white men, no anger toward them. Just hasn't happened, that's all. There's just never been an opportunity for me to deal with a white man on any kind of really tight level, physical or anything else. But I've always been curious about how a white man would treat me. I mean, would he be any different toward me than a black man? I've run into some difficult times with black men, so I've always wondered if things might be different with a white man. Maybe I've just let myself become a tool to the men I've been involved with. There have been three men in three years, and it's always been the same. I became too convenient for them. I guess I just give all of myself to whomever I'm involved with, and it's taken for granted. I've been badly misused.

I've got some friends who've dated white men, and I hear from these girls that they're treated beautifully, that they're made to feel quite feminine, like a queen. I think every woman wants to feel like a queen. I know I do. I know some black girls who wouldn't want anything *but* a white man. So I do get curious.

()

The black athlete tends to be almost worse than the white one in these bars where the players go after a game. Like, the black guy will kind of look at you out of the corner of one eye, as if to say: "What are you here for?" This is bad. Bad. You feel like you're being put in a category where you don't want to be placed. And don't forget, if the black man doesn't approach you, the white man won't. I don't know if the white guy is afraid to approach you because the black brother is there—or, because the white doesn't want to be conspicuous and stand out like a sore thumb.

Listen, it's very hard for a black woman to go to *any* bar by herself. If I'm in the mood to have a drink sometime, let's say, I have to think twice about just walking into a bar alone.

A white woman would be much more at ease doing this, because the white man will talk to her. But the first thing a black woman gets in a situation like that is a question mark: what are you coming here for? You know, what's your bag? Are you a professional? A white woman professional could go into the same place but not get the same kind of looks. But if you're black, they think you must have a *purpose*. She's just more rejected than the white. And maybe it's this simple, maybe this is mainly why you don't see as many black girls with athletes as whites; because the black woman is hesitant about going places, about making what seems like an aggressive approach to an athlete, black or white. I mean, if you do go and behave at all out of the ordinary, you get those looks out of corners of the eye. You know, what do you expect from a black woman?

I think that a lot of white guys would like to walk up to you and say something. If you look pretty decent, a man is usually going to act like a man; he'd say hello or something. But if he sees you sitting there alone, he may think you've got a hook out with some bait on it. He doesn't want to be the fish, so he's not going to approach you. A black woman just can't be accepted on the same level as another woman. And that really bothers me. I hate to be categorized. Don't hang a jacket on me: know me first. But if you don't know me, don't try and put an emphasis on how or what I am.

It would be nice to be part of this atmosphere, even just to get a little friendship out of these situations. I was just lucky to meet Billy the way I did, because most of these athletes just sit up on their king's throne and sort of say: "Here I am. You either come to me or else." And this is the battle the black women have to fight with the black man.

Now personally, I've never gone to any of these sports bars alone because I'm not looking for somebody. I'm not out to put myself on anybody, to catch an athlete. And you know, most black women just really don't know where these places are. Unless they're taken, they just don't go.

And these places tend to be a lot more fun for white women because the black athletes are most inclined to dig the white women anyway. So why should I go and expose myself to an insult. Can't do that if you think anything of yourself at all.

()

In the atmosphere of a sports bar, I think that white women have more of an aggressive way: they're more outgoing in these situations. They seem to get right in the middle of everything—the conversations, whatever is going on in the bar. And the black woman just sits, kind of dumbfounded, watching. Maybe you can add a word or two to whatever's said, but you hold it back. You start to feel that if you talk too much, or even just a little, you'll be accused of butting in. You can't become a part of the group in a situation like this mainly because the black man hasn't made you feel like you can participate, as if you really belong in this bar. He hasn't made you feel comfortable there.

My athlete friend wouldn't introduce me to any of these other athletes. He would just pick himself up and kind of table hop and just leave me sitting there alone, feeling uncomfortable. Somebody would come up to our table, and my guy would just get up and talk to the person and not include me. So when I'd see this person at another gig, I still wouldn't know them. I'd still be unable to relax. I just can't impose myself on someone in a situation like that. It's the man's duty.

It doesn't have anything to do with black-white people things either. I have confidence in myself. I consider myself as good as anyone—whatever color. I tell you what: I don't feel *better* than anyone, but I don't feel that anyone is better than me. That's where I stand. People have tried to make me feel that they're better than me, but it doesn't work.

O

Billy never took me to any of these football orgy parties
I've heard about. I'm sure he would go, but not with me. I've
never been to any kind of orgy, but I'm sure it might be a gas.
(Laughs.) It wouldn't have taken much to make an orgy out
of some of the parties we did go to. Some of the players could
really put the booze away; they'd sure get in a different mood
away from the football field. They were changed people away
from the game. They seemed to be relaxing their minds into a
different kind of excitement. People in the public eye have to
do that because of all the pressure on them. When you get
out of everybody's eyesight, you tend to do what you really
want to do in some kind of sacred seclusion—drinking,
dancing, hitting on a broad, but a different way when you're
alone. And that's how these stars get off into different bags.
They try to have a *new* kind of good time.

Nobody ever approached me at these parties, but I saw it
happen with other girls there. You know, a player coming up
to a girl and saying, "Mama, I would like to lay you." And
that's not a right approach to a lady. I just carry myself in a
certain way, and I don't get this kind of thing. It's all in your
manner, I think.

O

Billy was sitting at the other end of the bar. I'd just come
from a modeling job and was having a drink with a girlfriend.
He looked a little lost, and dazed, but he kept staring at us.
Polite staring. After a bit, he walked over and started talking
to us, or mostly to me, I mean. He asked where I worked and
things like that, but he never talked about who he was or
what he did. I didn't know he was a famous athlete until he
came to see me at my office about a week later.

He asked me if I knew anything about football, or about
his team. I really didn't: I didn't care that much about

sports. But I had heard of him. There had been some negative talk about him, about his adventures with women, so at first I kind of withdrew. I didn't want to get involved with someone who had a reputation of forcing himself on women.

But he kept calling and dropping by the office, and after I got to know him I started feeling differently about him. He didn't come on all that strong with me. Not until the end, and even then not that badly.

He was strange, though. His approach to me was different than other men. It was like he was trying to learn all he could about me before letting me know who he was. I began to feel that he was an okay guy. He wasn't as bad as his publicity.

The first night we went out he wanted me to stop at his apartment with him. But I wouldn't. His reputation was still in the back of my mind. He didn't make an issue of it. He just said that he wanted me to feel comfortable. I was almost sure he knew that I'd heard something about him.

About the fourth or fifth time we went out, he decided to go by his place for some beer. And we did. He didn't approach me with any big sexual advances. He started out very smooth and calm, and I guess it all just kind of progressed into sex. If he had pushed it too hard too early, he would have scared me off.

0

I can't sit here and tell you that Billy and I ever went to bed together. There was really no bed. (Giggles.) It may seem kind of weird in a way—and, like I say, he's nice people—but his thing was to have sex on the floor. He liked the floor. Not that he *insisted* you get right down there on the rug. He just kind of motivated you down that way. He would guide you that way. Whether we were at his place or in a hotel, he came up with the same type of action.

The first time it happened, I didn't give too much thought to it because we'd been sitting on the floor watching television. And all of a sudden, it happened. We'd just been sitting on pillows on the floor, drinking beer and watching TV, and it happened. He kissed me, and it went from there, right on the floor. Seems now like sort of an obscene thing. Not *that* obscene, because I guess that's where he dug it. I mean, I had done it on the floor before, but not *all* the time. (Laughs.)

He was a very sexy man. he never came on abruptly. He worked his way up to things. Worked *you* up to things, which I think is beautiful. He was concerned about how you felt, whether you were comfortable and enjoying things. He would sometimes stop and say, "You enjoying yourself, baby?" I just didn't expect this out of Billy. I thought he might be like a barbarian or something.

He reminded me quite a bit of my last husband. Both had the same sign, Scorpio. They were different people, sure, but when it came to sex they were basically the same: pleasers. And I dug that. Not that Billy was better sexually than my ex-husband: but he definitely wasn't worse. Scorpios are definitely lovers.

My orgasms with him were close to the top of the peak in my experience. Always had one with him, and he was always concerned that I did make it; he wanted to be sure I did.

His own response was different than most men. As he came close to a climax, he'd get kind of rough like. And I think that's why he always was concerned about how I felt while this was going on. He wanted to make sure I was all right. And I was not scared, just quite relaxed. I did wonder sometimes, though, if this roughness of his was going to get worse.

I mean, you hear a man howling almost like a wolf and you do wonder a little bit. I mean, he hollered; sounds, words, moans, groans. Nothing obscene. Just these moans and groans that would get louder and louder. Things you kind of expect anyway, but louder. Let's face it; when you're having sex, when you're approaching a climax, you let some sounds out. It's kind of difficult to hold them in. But his sounds were just more harsh than normal. I got the feeling that Billy was just more open with it, more honest with his noises. And actually, I kind of like men's noises anyway. When you hear them, you know they're enjoying what you've done for them. I'm not an aggressive person, but when I'm having sex with someone I do get aggressive. I don't mind asking my man to have sex if I'm in that mood. If he's asleep, I'll wake him up. I'm aggressive when I know that this man belongs to me. Yet, I didn't get too agressive with Billy at first. I was leery, you know. I didn't want to turn him on right away, because I didn't know what I might be turning him on *to*.

He would always sit and watch me for a long time. He kept telling me that I was a different kind of woman for him. He would look and then he would take his hand and, very softly, go over my entire body, as if he was trying to see if I had any physical imperfections. He'd go from my toes to my head with a great deal of admiration, like he had to visualize in his mind, through touching, what he was really getting involved with. No man had ever done that with me before. Maybe Billy wasn't really looking for my defects; maybe this was a way of turning himself on looking, feeling, squeezing, kissing over my body.

I kind of felt that he really dug me, that he didn't do this with every woman. I felt that maybe I was kind of special to him.

'chicago shirley'...
a <u>mensch</u> of a nymph

NOTE: Baseball's most durable, most celebrated Bimbo is known to the athletes only as Chicago Shirley. Somebody, presumably her husband, knows her real name. I was on the brink of a trip to Chicago to hunt down Shirley, but first decided to ask a Chicago sports columnist for clues. While we chatted in the press box of the Oakland Coliseum, Reggie Jackson was examining the product of Wilbur Wood.

"What's Shirley's favorite bar?" I asked the columnist.

"Doesn't matter anymore," he said. "She's dead."

At that moment Reggie homered off Wilbur. I wasn't certain I'd heard the columnist.

Chicago Shirley dead?

"Died eighteen months ago," he said.

"Are you sure?"

He was sure.

So I forgot my trip to Chicago and decided instead to tell the Chicago Shirley story via a ballplayer who'd been serviced by her. Finding the knowledgeable athlete took virtually seconds. He is an active, excellent American Leaguer. An All-Star, in fact. He was at first hesitant to reveal his store of Shirleyana but finally agreed that posterity needed such an accounting.

Two months later, after the player had been in Chicago, he came to me with a sweet smile and the news that Shirley lived yet.

"Are you sure?"

He was sure. Very sure.

Perhaps, I suggested, we leave well enough alone; we view her through the heart of a young man who once cared very much.

He agreed. "Anyway," he said, "she hasn't changed."

And so, not in memoriam....

chicago shirley... *At least forty-years-old; kind of fat with short, light brown hair; a high school history teacher in Greater Chicagoland; married to a six-foot, six-inch tall suburban policeman. ("Guess he wasn't enough for her.") She weighed about one-hundred-fifty pounds, stood about five feet, seven inches tall; she loved baseball, knew everybody's record—"how many hits they had and everything"; would get contentious when loaded.*

When I first came up to the majors, I heard from some of the older players on my team about all the guys going out with her. On my first trip into Chicago, a teammate introduced me to her in a bar-place near our hotel called The Inkwell. I knew I'd be taken care of by her if I wanted to. She wanted to meet all the players. This other player and I sat and talked with her. I expected to see something a little better than her. I couldn't believe it. This *fat* woman. But she seemed pleasant, nice to get along with. We had two or three drinks, and that was it.

I went back to our hotel. Cause I was a rookie and still a kid, nineteen or so, they had me rooming with the team's batboy. He was only fifteen. When I get to the room, there's a phone call from this player I was with at the bar. He said he had a girl for me. I said, "Not Shirley?" He sort of laughed and told me no.

Well, a few minutes later there was a knock on the door. And in came running one player with women's panties on and another player with a woman's slip on and then Shirley completely nude. She was at least as fat nude as she was in clothes. Some players said she used to be fatter.

The two players left, and so there were me and the batboy in the room with a naked Shirley. We had twin beds, and I told her to take care of the batboy first. She hopped right on top of him. I think he was a virgin. When she finished, I remember him saying: "What will my mother think?" Nothing she did that night, or ever, surprised me.

After she finished with the batboy, she hopped right on me. Just jumped right over on my bed. It was pure nymphomania. I had never seen a nymphomaniac before. As far as I can remember, she orgasmed with both of us. It couldn't have lasted too long. I was so young then. I just figured I'd get my happiness and that's it.

When we were in Chicago after that I'd knock her off once in a while—unless I had another girl. If you were with another girl and Shirley saw you, she'd walk right on by. She wouldn't nag on you. And she'd fix up me and other ball players with other girls if we wanted. For years she did that. She knew when a player wanted a girl and when he didn't. She really had an eye for a horny guy. She could look at five or six players sitting around drinking together and she could pick out the one guy who wanted to mess around. But if she was the only girl in a bar with a lot of men she'd get on the phone and get some girls into the place.

I guess there were certain players she liked more than others. When one of the guys on our team was sent down, she'd follow him around at minor league games when his team was playing close to Chicago. I heard she had a book with the name of every guy in the American League she'd laid. I heard she was trying to get the name of every guy in the league in the book. But I never asked her about that book.

If nothing else was available in Chicago, I'd screw Shirley. As a lay, she wasn't bad. She might not have been the prettiest thing in the world, but she knew what she was doing. And there was no player that didn't know exactly what she wanted.

One trip into Chicago, Shirley phoned me about a girl she'd fixed me up with once. She told me I'd knocked up this girl. But she said the girl said it was half her fault and half mine. Shirley said she gave the girl money for an abortion, and that I owed her a hundred-fifty dollars. I didn't think she'd lie. So I borrowed the money from our trainer and went over and gave Shirley the hundred fifty.

A FOOTNOTE TO SHIRLEY (S): Detroit also has a Shirley, known to athletes as Detroit Shirley. And New York used to have a Shirley, too. She operated out of one midtown hotel and was known as (hotel deleted) Shirley. Detroit Shirley obviously covered more ground—and may still—than her counterparts. A Detroit sportswriter says that "His Shirley" told him she sprinkled favors in three cities in a period of five days midway through the 1972 baseball season. He saw her in two of those cities and believes every word. She was keenly active, he says, at the 1972 All-Star Game headquarters in Atlanta. He saw her collecting room keys. It must have been like Mecca for Detroit Shirley.

New York's Shirley was a white running back fetishist. My informant, not a white running back, says that N.Y. Shirley just *had* to service as many white running backs as possible before either football or she died. A visiting Texas professional team learned of her needs, and its courier promised New York Shirley an evening with the club's most prominent white running back. She couldn't have been more appreciative of the courier's concern. That evening, Shirley arrived in the pre-designated hotel room—in her hotel, of course—and had barely inched open the door when she heard a voice coming out of the darkness from the direction of what seemed to be a bed. The voice asked her to leave the lights off, and, please, hurry. The voice said it couldn't wait. Nor could New York Shirley. It was over quickly. The lights went on, and Shirley found herself under a running back from that team all right—a black running back. Several players had hidden in the room and at the moment of truth and lightness blared out, "Surprise!"

halftime stuff

DEAR DR. REUBEN: Now that tennis has become such a popular sport, I wonder if there is any relation between being a good tennis player and being a good sexual partner. I'm really serious about this because the men who are good at tennis seem to have such a sexy way about them—and I know I'm not the only woman who feels this way.

ANSWER: Tennis is an athletic event—and so is sex. Generally anything that improves a person's athletic ability also improves their sexual ability....

...From Dr. David Reuben's syndicated newspaper column of August 5, 1973.

I've been on two major league teams. I'd say that on each, twenty-two of the twenty-five guys messed around. I understand why. Ballplayers are like any other men. They have very delicate egos. They're basically insecure of their manhood. But there are degrees of messing. It's how it's done. Sometimes just for the company, okay. But I don't dig the kind of guy who shows no respect for his real woman, his wife or his sweetheart. That's the worst

*degree of messing. Your woman must be respected. On
one of our road trips the families were permitted to come
along. And while this guy's wife was up there in the
hotel, I saw him necking with another broad in an alley
half a block away. That's the utmost.*
—*A bachelor outfielder.*

the little yellow butterfly

maggie... *twenty-five-years old, five feet seven inches tall, one hundred thirty pounds—short, dark hair, and eyes she describes as "golden."...mother, with whom she lived after parents' early divorce, was "incredibly athletic" and once moonlighted as a bookmaker...product of parochial schooling, later taught physical education at a Catholic grammar school...married at eighteen to high school sweetheart, divorced three years later. In between, lost a four-day-old baby...slept with twenty-one baseball players—most of them married pitchers and two of them blacks—in one season. Known to major leaguers as a "dynamite blow jobber."...A younger brother played baseball and football with her. "A lot of people told me when I was younger that I should have been a boy," she says. "I do have feelings that I'm more masculine than feminine. I'd never be a lesbian, though."...Attended several colleges, worked several jobs, including hospital clerk and cocktail waitress...a small daisy is tattooed over her abundant left breast. The daisy, she says, is a "symbol of participation." On her right thigh is tattooed a little yellow butterfly, which symbolizes nothing but does serve to call attention to an attractive right thigh...hopes to turn hobbies of writing and photography into a pictorial about pitchers pitching and screwing...does not consider herself a sports groupie. "I would never want to make any of my relationships with the ballplayers a joke," she says. "I'm sure most of the ballplayers I've been with don't joke about me like I've heard them talk about Chicago Shirley or Detroit Shirley. I don't see myself as the Shirley of this town. No way. I'm not open*

for every *ballplayer." ... Maintains a ledger on her*
sexual experiences with baseball players, and her own
feelings about the game. An excerpt:

When my skin turns to golden brown. When my hair
dances with the sunlight and the smile on my face
becomes permanent. When my mornings begin at six a.m.,
out of want, and my body becomes alive and longing.
When I feel that I can wait no longer, Opening Day finally
arrives. My long winter is over, my summer has come, and
this winter bud becomes a flower wild with delight and
passion for the men that play this marvelous game of
baseball.

All Star names become my breath. My weeks are
divided between American and National, my days are no
longer Mondays or Tuesdays, but series. My nights
become innings.

In a stadium alive with people, I become singular. But
my oneness allows me to capitalize on the pulsating
sensations escaping from the men who make up this breed
of athletes. Their excitement stimulates my own. The
gracefulness in their bodies only distracts me.

They are beauties with mesmerizing legs. Legs that
pitch, legs that catch, legs that hit; running legs, strong,
solid legs, legs that ache, legs that are abused, but legs that
also hint sensuously, longingly for a different type of
game.

This is the game that begins after the last out is made.
This is the game that makes their performances on the
field anti-climatic. This is the game they *never* lose. This is
the other ball game.

Men are so hung up on penis sizes and balling ability. The
first question every man asks me is who's the best. I mean,
ballplayers who know everybody else. Or who's got the
biggest cock. It's ridiculous.

I remember that this superstar baseball bachelor once told
me that one of his relief pitchers could knock me from wall to
wall without a hard-on. It's not important. And by the end of

my first big season in baseball, I was trying to convey to all
these guys that it was not that important, because the
players asked me the same repetitive questions continuously.
   Men are funny. It's that big male ego thing. Each of them
would like me to tell them that they're the best hung and
that they're the best in bed. And I do tell most of them that
when I'm with *them*. But naturally I'm prejudiced toward
the ones I really like, too, because they're lovers. And the
best real, true lover of all of them was the one manager I had
that season. He was incredible. He once even sent me flowers.
It was really very nice. And the first athlete I ever balled, an
N.B.A. guy, also sent me flowers. Just those two.

()

   I was working on a paper for a college class and needed
some photographs of athletes, so I went up to the mountains
to this celebrity golf tournament. I guess when you get down
to it, I really went up there to see Joe Namath, to
photograph him. But I ended up spending all the time with
this married basketball superstar, and the funny thing is that
when I met him, I didn't know who he was. I wasn't into
basketball too much then, although now it's my second
favorite sport. Next to baseball, of course. That was my first
physical encounter with an athlete, even though to this day I
never think of the basketball player as being this great star
he is. I never can think of him as just an athlete, but maybe
that's because I was more naive at the time I met him. But
meeting him then was nothing like seeing Joe Namath—who
was my hero.
   I was just standing there taking pictures, and the
basketball player asked me to have lunch between the two
sets of holes. I said yes, and it didn't even phase me. All I
knew about this guy was that he must have been an athlete;
their bodies always give them away. Meanwhile, I did take
pictures of Joe Namath, and he did autograph an old New

York Jet T-shirt I'd been saving for years. But that was all. I was not impressed with Namath, but still he was my hero. And he will be. Always.

After lunch, the basketball player invited me out to dinner, and again I agreed. Later, a caddy told me the player's name. Then it finally sunk in who he was, and I said to myself, "Oh, wow."

We ended up going to bed for the rest of the golf tournament. That's all we did. (Laughs.) He was an incredible man, a real thoughtful person because he always took time to talk to me and stuck with me the whole time, too, even though he didn't have any reason to.

In bed, he wasn't into his trip. He was interested in giving me as much pleasure as I was giving him. He had an uncanny way of knowing when I wanted to go to bed—even when we were on the golf course. He'd look at me and say, "Not right now." He didn't have too many qualms about being seen with the same girl constantly.

It was amazing the response he got from the crowds at the tournament, because his club had just won the N.B.A. championship, and people were coming up telling him how fantastic he was. Then they'd see me later and ask me for my autograph, and I didn't know what to do. So I just started signing them as his wife. I felt like such an important person, and that was hard to come down from afterwards—not being with just any athlete but with a superstar, which he definitely was, and still is. There are few people like him in his sport.

For those few days, I was constantly in the spotlight. It was very hard for me to come back home and go to work and school. I thought, what am I doing working as an admitting clerk in a hospital? That spotlight was incredible.

In thinking back now about that first time, I wonder what might have happened if it really had been Namath, but then I know that I never would have been able to go to bed with *him,* I idolized him too much. Anything like that would have shattered my image of him. Two guys I could never go to bed with are Joe Namath and Pete Rose. They're just too much of my heroes for that. Being that for me they're fantasy people, I don't want them brought down to a human level like all the other athletes I've been to bed with.

Anyway, now I'm not into football that much. I don't like the impact it's had on our society. It makes me sad. The game has become such a social event for the fans that they don't really care anymore what goes on on the field. They like to come to a game and they like to leave the game. What happens before and after the actual playing is more important. Football gives the fan a chance to release any violent feelings, and that's all. They just want to be part of something without really participating. They want to be part of a professional football team. But how can they? For that matter, it's easier to be part of a baseball team.

()

The basketball guy was just like any other man: he got great pleasure out of oral sex. Almost all men do. Most men I know—athletes or not—enjoy oral sex, however athletes are more honest. They're here for three days and gone, so they're more outright. They'll just say, well, hey, I dig that. But a non-athlete will have more patience because he's going to come see you again. But it's amazing how many men freeze at a woman who takes the initiative like that—which I do, which is why I get along so well with athletes. That's probably why they come back.

That's my way. My approach is usually orally first. I'm just not inhibited about that at all. I had a very good teacher. He was a minor league ballplayer who I met at a bar when I was working as a cocktail waitress. He couldn't stand a lot of the hassle and bullshit about baseball, so he left and became a bartender. The place we worked was one of those liberal beer-wine-rock joints, and I was the first girl he met there who he could talk to about sports, so we just developed a close relationship both sexually and as friends. We're still the best of friends, and sometimes it's still torrid even though he knows what else I go through.

I don't know how or what most women do when they give oral sex, but I know they must not do as well as I do. It's a matter of how far you can take a cock into your mouth without gagging; also what you do with your tongue while you have the guy in your mouth. It's not just a matter of sucking and nothing else. The important thing, the big thing about it is that you have to like it. If you don't like it, it's like balling. If you don't like balling, you're gonna lay there. But if you really dig it, you can get into doing that. And I have no qualms at all about someone coming in my mouth. That doesn't even bother me. Never did either. It must have been natural for me, because I took to it immediately.

I'd had some experience with it before I met the minor leaguer, but it was not good at all. I was very, very uptight when I was married because I'd just left a parochial high school. And I was pregnant, too, so there were inhibitions. But it has not been like that since.

I don't actually have a physical orgasm myself when I'm going down on a guy, but I get satisfaction because I'm taking the initiative. Because I'm being dominant. Maybe it's an envy, too. It's a pleasure for me.

Let me just give you an example of this one pitcher I know who really loves oral sex. He's a well-endowed male, too. He's huge, and he's probably one of the harder men I've had that I do that to. But I can do it, and I do it because even if it starts hurting—there's no way to stop the mandibles from tightening—I am delighted to watch the incredible pleasure he gets. He rewards me with the satisfaction that he does get pleasure.

()

The first time it happened with him was in this little house near a duck blind. There were five ballplayers and me in the place to begin with, but then three of them went out. My pitcher and I were laying in a bunk bed, and the other player who stayed was eating and reading a paper (laughs) while I was administering this blow job. The other player would look over at us for a second and then go back to reading his paper—although I wasn't paying much attention to *him*.

When I was finished, my pitcher said to the other guy, "Bunkie, I've had good blow jobs in my life, but that was *major league.*" I'm sure that's why the pitcher was interested in me—even though conversationally we got along well. Our personalities matched, you know. But I'm sure that he kept seeing me mainly for the way I gave him blow jobs.

That same day I ended up balling two other players there. With one of them I was so uptight, because he had this sexy air about him—like Burt Reynolds or Richard Harris. Then I realized that there were still two more guys there who hadn't gotten any sex that day, and I suddenly said to myself, "Wait a minute." I had never done this kind of thing before—balled more than one guy in one day. In my life, I had never done that. I mean, sex was always a very personal thing to me. It really is, and it still is. I become inhibited in a group. I would rather be alone with someone where I'm totally *un*inhibited.

So when this next player approached me that day, I said, "Aw, no. I don't know what's happening." And it took a while for him to accept that rejection. I explained to him later that it was not a rejection of him but a rejection of the whole idea. I mean, I thought it was just going to be two players at the duck blind originally, but a lot more showed up.

I went back to the duck blind a few more times. The sexy guy couldn't make it again for wife reasons, so things just got personal between me and the pitcher.

()

I know I said before that I envied the satisfaction the pitcher got when I blew him, but I didn't mean that I wanted to change places with him, that I wanted to *be* him. I mean, just being myself is where I fit. I've had climaxes taking the passive role, too, a lot. I come very easily. It's amazing how easily I come, so I've never worried about that.

But about this envy stuff, let me put it this way: the duck blind pitcher is about the most honest man sexually that I've ever met. He has no qualms about saying that he's satisfied, or telling me that the blow job was great. He cares about letting you know you're good. And a lot of athletes need this ego support—they all have big egos—and want to feel that it was they who were great and not you. But I know differently. I really do. I know I give a great blow job.

A lot of these guys call me again and want to take me to other towns. I know what they want, but I also know I have a lot more to offer than just a good blow job. With me, they can have a good rapport, too. I mean, I do feel that the first time together we're just using each other as sexual objects, but I don't feel that way the second time. I don't feel like that when a guy keeps me with him for several days.

You're no longer just a sexual object; he's got to like you, and I'm flattered by that. I'm flattered that I'm treated with that type of respect.

With them I'm a different person than I am with the normal man. With just a regular date, and I tend to date mostly professional men like doctors, I tend to exploit the fact that I'm an athlete. I contend I still am, because I continue to work at track and field. So with regular dates, I talk about it much more, I blow it up, I'm establishing where I'm at to them. But when I'm with the athlete, I don't have to establish that and I really feel I become more womanly. Much more womanly. The athletes will always be much more interesting to me than *I* will ever be to me, so I don't want to hear myself talking about me to them.

Most of the time there's not even much talk with athletes about sports unless I ask questions. We get more into feelings about things. I've gotten into some good relationships with about three athletes—the kind of relationships I didn't want to happen, because they hurt me now. Real affectionate relationships. I know I was in love with this one baseball player. He's not happily married, and it's incredible how compatible we are. It's funny that my duck blind pitcher knows this guy well. He was surprised that he wasn't divorced yet. He told me the guy's marriage was on the rocks years ago. And I guess it still is, but these athletes stick to their wives for some reason. I know a lot of unhappily married athletes who just stick it out.

()

I'd like to be married to an athlete. I like the idea of their going away, of having enough time of my own to do my own thing because I have a lot of interests of my own. I'm taking ballet right now. I want to continue with my college courses, and things like that. I like to be independent. And I know I can be faithful to one man. That's what happened to me after my first season with baseball players: I stayed faithful to just the guys I cared about, and nobody else impressed me.

I'm not saying I couldn't meet some baseball superstar tomorrow and not go to bed with him. Sure, because I have natural reactions to men, but on certain clubs I will only go to bed with a certain guy, and nobody else. I'm involved enough just with them. I do like men, but I don't want to lay them all. Maybe if I decide to write my own book, I will get into more of them. I took some notes in my first season, but not enough, because I was too naive, too impressed.

()

I don't like sportswriters. I do not favor them at all; they're prejudiced against me immediately because I aspire to do what *they're* doing. It's incredible the way they think.

91   *maggie*

I don't think it's because they're jealous of me or that they consider me a threat. They just seem to take the attitude: Ah, is she kidding? It's sort of a very masculine bigotry. There's this one sportswriter from the Midwest who heard me talking about baseball one night. And he sat back and looked at me like I didn't know what I was talking about, that I had read it all somewhere and couldn't possibly know all of these things about the game myself. That's what I mean. I just don't get on with writers.

Remember, too, that the sportswriters' experiences end where mine can start. That's a whole different story for them. I can get to know athletes the way a writer never can—in a much more personally revealing way. When I'm with an athlete, there's no shield there, no big shot ego trip. Just the ballplayer as a man.

()

I don't like the word "groupie" or "Baseball Annie" applied to me. I just think that athletes are a beautiful breed of men, so one of my ideas is to do a pictorial. I don't think there's anything more beautiful than a pitcher when he's pitching a game. That sight is so lovely, so beautiful to me that the first time I ever took pictures at a game of a pitcher, I almost got into it enough to have an orgasm. Just watching him work.

I have orgasms easily, as I said. The sun happens to be a constant lover of mine. That's a sensitivity thing for me, and it's almost the same when I watch a pitcher doing well. But sometimes I get very tearful—not because of the man who's pitching but because *I* can't do it myself, because I'm encompassed by a female body that will eliminate my doing something that is really fantastic. So what I have to do is find my own sports, track and field and tennis. But I love baseball. I have had an orgasm just watching a ball game. I have an incredible imagination. My mind can do wonderful things for my body. I can get off easy, without touching myself. It's hard and it has to be just the right time. But it happens.

When I'm watching a pitcher, I go from this teary-eyed thing to thinking about the pitcher himself; whether I've been to bed with him or not doesn't really matter. I watch their legs—that really turns me on. I happen to be a leg person. The thigh muscles particularly. That's the first thing I look at. The basketball player I mentioned just had the most beautiful legs I've ever seen. I mean really. I just admire that in those men; they're so developed. And now my leg muscles are starting to develop from running and walking and exercising them so much.

()

His picture was on the cover of a national sports magazine, and for the only time in my life I told myself that I had to have *a* guy. I definitely set out to meet him.

The whole week had been confusing. I was standing in line in my tennis outfit waiting to buy basketball tickets when I met this pitcher from a visiting club and ended up spending a couple days at his hotel with him, but not balling him. When his team left, cover boy's team came to the same hotel, and I was still in a room there. I had to be with this guy. His masculinity popped right out at me from that picture. And in the lobby the very first night his team was in town, I did meet him. Not only is he great looking, but he's a fantastic ballplayer, too.

At first when we were talking, he was very nice—until the line of conversation tended toward sex. I didn't blatantly bring up the subject; it was sort of a double connotative thing. But once we got on that subject, cover boy became like a split personality. He got very, very dirty. I guess the only reason I ended up having sex with him was a sort of "Last Tango in Paris" aura: like, here's a man you can, damn, have sex with or whatever you want and then just tell him to leave. You know, just out and out sex without caring if he said *anything* to me.

But he had different ideas. He wanted a group thing.

He and some other guys on his team told me that I hadn't balled anybody until I balled one of their pitchers because he had such a big cock. So I did, but not just because of that. I'd met him earlier in the evening and I liked his looks. He did have a big cock, though. Yes, he did. But it made no difference. That's a fallacy.

Cock size is not important to me at all, but I must point out that every athlete I've balled has been well-endowed. There are just some that are more endowed than the others, compared to non-athletes I've dated that aren't so big. I think the size all has to do with the way they develop their body and the physical work they do. I would think that construction workers might be the same way—men that do physical labor. There's a circulation that's much stronger. Or, maybe I've just been lucky and got all the goodies.

After I finished balling the pitcher with the big cock, I was ready to leave and forget about cover boy, but he caught me in the hallway and asked me to come down to his room. When we got there, he leaned back on his bed with a drink in one hand and a cigarette in the other. I mean, this man wanted nothing but oral sex. He didn't want me to even get undressed; he didn't want to get undressed himself. He wanted it right there. Incredibly egotistical.

I told him that I was not a whore, that I was not doing this for bread. While I was talking to him, another pitcher from his club walked in, and cover boy says, "Honey, if you can't blow us both, you can't have me." That was his exact attitude.

I said, "No, sir. You don't mean anything to me."

I was going to leave, but I couldn't find my shoes, which I always remove the minute I get in a room. I even take them off at the ballpark. Well, I finally did find my shoes, and was starting to get up and go when cover boy got very rough and put his hands around my neck. I did want to ball him, but I didn't want any of this instant blow job stuff. I wanted *my* pleasure, too.

He moved his hands from my neck to my head; he wasn't choking me or anything, just holding me hard. And he stared at me for the longest time. I could have had an orgasm right then. There's a little masochism in everybody, I think. I was afraid that his sexual attraction was overwhelming.

He knew I had a camper, and he said, "Let's go out in your car."

So I took him out to the camper. That was a mistake, because he wanted the same thing in the camper, and I did it—with not very much pleasure and almost under forcible measures.

I did it—and it was on the bed part of the camper—because he was being so obstinate and mean that I wanted to show him it didn't matter. I mean, I was trying to prove something, and in essence it failed. We both just literally fucked each other's heads. That's all we did. All I did was give him a blow job, and it took a few minutes because he'd been drinking a lot. But no kind words were passed after it was over. I was really bitter, so bitter that I wrote in my notebook that I never wanted anything more to do with any ballplayers ever again. That was the misstatement of the year. Next day, another team came to town and greeted me very warmly.

A couple of months after I did my thing in the camper with cover boy, his club came back to town. I was sitting in a baseball bar when I saw cover boy walk in, so I turned my back and started talking to another guy on his team—and he turned out to be a bummer, too. I've given that club my "Most Valuable Perverts—MVP—Award." That's my opinion of them.

This latest player of theirs took me back to his hotel room, which I consented to, you know, and within five minutes ten other guys from his club walked in.

I said, "What the *hell* is this?"

One of them took me out of that room and down to his. But they all followed us. I finally said to myself, "Screw this," and I left. I never want anything to do with *that* team again. Not with anybody on that team. And they all know me, too. It's amazing how quick word travels. Amazing.

I have a baseball that most of the major league teams know about. It was awarded to me by a relief pitcher. Most relief pitchers in both leagues know me because when I would take pictures I would always shoot them warming up in the bullpen. Then I stayed in a seat behind the bullpen. When I couldn't get near the field, I would shoot from the bullpen because that's the closest I could get with the kind of camera lens I had. It was really an inadequate lens.

The ball was given to me—according to that relief pitcher—for being "The Most Valuable Beaver Shot in the Game."

()

In hot weather, I never wear underwear. No hose either. Nothing underneath. I have this thing with the sun, and I have to have it on my body. And I really think that not wearing underwear in the summer has saved me from having a lot of female problems. Yeast infections and those things. I wear fairly short skirts, too. Not micro-minis, but fairly short.

This one over-hot night, I went to a game to shoot and was standing on a high platform right near the players' entrance to the field. And I guess I was standing at just the right angle or something—especially when I stooped over to get equipment out of my camera bag. Not that my skirt went up or anything, but just the angle that the players could see when they were coming up from behind me. I turned around once and saw this hotshot bachelor pitcher stopped dead in his tracks and staring at me. A good-looking guy, too.

He says to me, "C'mere. Hey, c'mere." And I did.

He says, "The last thing a man expects to see on his way to the bullpen is a woman's bare ass. What are you doing after the game?" A pitcher on the local team had warned me about messing around with this other guy, too. He said he was trouble. But the guy's comment just seemed to hit me well (laughs), so I went and had a drink with him. And he turned out to be a real ass.

As soon as we were in the bar—I guess he couldn't wait—he made a grab for me. The idea that I didn't have any underpants on must have been too much for him. He had to get back to the hotel room right away. And he laid this on me: "I've got to pitch tomorrow, so I can't have you staying around too late."

Can you believe this? That man balled, and that was it. I mean, unless I was a dumb, dumb woman there could be no other way to take that. It was obvious that he wanted me to leave right after balling. He got up and started putting on his pajamas, so I left. Believe me, I'll never go out with that pitcher again.

I went from his room down to the lobby and started talking with two other guys from his team. This is crazy, but it wasn't ten minutes before I went back upstairs into one of their rooms, and balled one of them. And I'll never know why. I guess it was because I felt I didn't get anything from the bigshot bachelor earlier. I didn't have an orgasm with him in that quickie.

Not that I just would have balled right away again with *any* man. If I hadn't bumped into this other player in the lobby, I could have gone right home and everything would have been fine. But this second guy was just a very nice guy. We had a very nice night together.

()

I know there isn't any question, I go mostly after pitchers. If I was to make a list of the baseball players I balled, most of the names on it would be pitchers. And nearly all of the names on the list are married ballplayers. The single guys are too hard to cope with. They feel they have something that every girl wants, and they're not willing to give it up.

One of the best-known single guys in sports once invited me to a golf tournament that was for a lot of different athletes. He had seen me only once, just conversationally and only for a couple of minutes. But then he called me and asked me to fly to this tournament. He wondered if it would be okay with my parents, and I kind of laughed and told him sure. I came to find out after I joined him that he thought I was nineteen years old, not over twenty-one.

And this guy turned out to be a very egotistical man when it comes to women. In the sports brotherhood, he's a good man. But not with women. The whole time we were at this tournament, he was looking at every other girl while every other man was looking at me. It was the most ridiculous couple of days. I just don't like that kind of treatment.

We were laying in bed one of the nights, and I told him that I'd really had it. I asked him if he could find out if one of the football players there I knew had his wife along. I told him I dug the football player, and he didn't understand my interest in another guy. The thing was, he'd finally met his match.

But he sure was a damned good screw. That's all I can say. He wasn't much of a preliminary man, but when he did it, man, he could *screw.* I mean, sometimes I can dig it like that. So as far as that goes, very seldom did I turn him down just for a ball. He's good, but not a good *lover,* because he's interested primarily in himself. And he does like younger girls more. They just have a more awesome attitude toward him. After the tournament was over, we said goodbye, and I knew that was it, that I'd never ball him again. And I haven't.

0

One of the few times I ever got soused at the ball park happened to be the same day I met this really great backup catcher. I was sitting behind the bullpen as usual, and it was one of the hottest days I can remember, so this stranger sitting next to me kept buying beers. He never stopped buying, and I never stopped looking at this bullpen catcher.

After the game, I went to the catcher's hotel room, and talk about getting it on... I mean, it didn't stop all night. The catcher's roommate is asleep in the other bed snoring while we were balling, but he never woke up. At least not until the phone rang. The roommate answered it finally. Apparently it was a girl he knew, and he talked to her about two, three hours while we kept balling a couple of feet away. It must have been very trying for the roommate to go through, but later I got to be good friends with him, too.

My catcher had to leave to visit some relatives in the area next morning, so I balled the roommate after breakfast. I did have guilt feelings, but he was so nice. There was no repercussion at all, though. In fact, the two of them call me their "third roommate."

They took me with them to the next town on their road trip, and I even ended up talking to their manager. Just talking to him. I guess he'd seen me from his balcony patio while I was nude in a whirlpool-type thing down below. Apparently he'd watched me slip off my brassiere when I got in the pool. He had his wife on the trip, and we just talked. That was all. But he did want to know if I was with any of his players. I told him I didn't feel at liberty to say. And that was that.

Another manager made a pitch to ball me once, but I turned him down. I just wasn't interested in him as a person. In that first season, though, I did have a relationship with a manager. *One* manager. A truly beautiful guy.

()

I was drinking with two pitchers from this club at a hotel bar when one of them looks around and says, "Oh, oh, the manager's in here, too. I better get up to bed." And he left.

But I wasn't alone for long, because a guy walked up who I knew from the local club. I'd had something going with him early in the season. But not that night, because he took me right over and introduced me to that manager. And the manager invited me to drink with him. It was hard for me to believe that a manager could be so good-looking. We drank and we talked and the bar closed and then there was just nothing said. I walked out of the bar with him right to his suite. I stayed with him that night and the next day and the next night. He was just a real gentleman.

I told him some of my stories about ballplayers, and he said he was going to have to teach me how to be particular. But by this time, I *was* starting to get particular.

There was nobody who could love like this manager. It was just the way he did things. He would never let me get undressed myself; he always did it and then put me in the shower. A manager, you know, always has an incredible suite, not just a room like a ballplayer. And he didn't have any hangups about being seen with me, either. Not in the lobby or the hotel bar even. And I think all the players looked at him admirably because of this.

It's a trip how all of his players respond to me now. Like this one pitcher of his who I'd been trying to get together with during earlier trips. Circumstances had kept us apart, but we really dug each other. Well, I thought I finally would be able to be with him on the club's last visit to town, but I told him I had to be in the manager's room later.

"Guess the manager comes first," he told me.

I said, "That's not necessarily true."

And he said, "You're really getting into the big time, huh?"

()

Toward the end of my first season, I guess you could say I made my longest road trip of the year. Went to one town with my bullpen catcher friend and then to two other cities with my pitcher friend from the duck blind and his ball club—I mean a *lot* of guys from his ball club.

After I left my catcher for the second town, my mind was already geared to what might happen, because I knew a lot of guys on the pitcher's club were interested. I was in the pitcher's room first, then he called two teammates and told them to come down to his room, too.

I balled one of them while the other two watched television, then I balled the third one in the bathroom. In the tub. I guess I was getting inhibited because I didn't want the other two guys to be in the same room this time. But even more than that, when I feel good rapport with someone—and I did with this third guy—I want to be alone with them. So we went into the bathtub. No water, and it was a little uncomfortable, although I think we ended up on the bathroom floor. Just to get away from the other two guys.

And then the pitcher who invited me on the trip left his room. He really spaced out on me. He ended up with a couple of other girls in this town, and I had to stay with two other players in their room. But before I moved out of the pitcher's room that night, another player from the club came in, and he was really loaded. He just staggered in, leaned against a partition and started getting undressed. This guy and I were just complete sexual partners; there was no need for any conversation. He balled me and walked right out of the room still with a hard-on and wearing only his T-shirt and underpants. He was so drunk he told another player the next day that he didn't even remember balling me.

So in the space of about three hours I blew one and balled three on this same team.

The next night I spent in the room with those two players I mentioned. They tried to be platonic, but I did ball one of them. They felt badly that the pitcher had sort of run out on me. But after one night with them, they thought it might be better if I stayed someplace else.

Another guy on the team wasn't using his room; he was out visiting relatives. So I slept in his room the final night in

101   *maggie*

town. Alone. By that time, I'd gotten into some heavy head trips on my own and started doubting what I was doing. And it finally started hitting me that I wasn't going to be seeing my bullpen catcher for a while.

I just can't forget how lonely I felt. That was some head trip I got into. I started realizing that all this pretending and all this fun that came from being surrounded by all these athletes just wasn't fulfilling.

I got very hysterical. I was crying one morning after breakfast, and I had enough medical experience to know that my body was reacting physically to a breakdown. Physically and emotionally. I was starting to hyperventilate; I was breathing very irregularly, and I could not control my crying.

One of the players saw me—one of the guys I'd balled on that trip—and said he'd take me to a doctor for tranquilizers. I was still crying without any control while we walked through the lobby. The other players saw me with this guy, and it must have been very embarrassing for him.

And there were some wives along on that trip, too, so I really felt encompassed by fear and loneliness. I'm also very sensitive. Blatant sex is only important to me sometimes. I'm an incurable romanticist. I like men. I mean, I *really* do. And it all hit me at once. The player did take me to a doctor for tranquilizers. Then, later, I had a quiet evening in the hotel bar with a few of the guys and I felt a little more relaxed. Several of them were just very nice and good to me.

That experience convinced me—for a little while anyway—that I shouldn't go on to the next town with this ball club. I decided it would be very bad for me to go. However, I did, and it wasn't too good.

0

My duck blind pitcher had told me in advance what he expected me to do in the last town. And this is really awful; this is one thing that I really regret, and always will, and hope that everybody's just laughing at it. He told me some of the players had planned a big party on this road trip and that one of them had the reputation for being a great "gobbler," a guy who had a fantastic way of going down on a woman, and who loved it. So it was planned in advance that he was going to go down on me at this party, in front of a dozen or so guys on the club—most of whom I already knew.

When the night of the party arrived, I told my pitcher that I really had to think about going ahead with his idea. And I started to drink a lot, which I rarely do.

I'm a Sagittarius, so naturally I psychoanalyze everything. I'm very philosophical. I had feelings that if I didn't let this guy go down on me, the pitcher would be upset with me, and I wasn't strong enough to take rejection of any kind right then—even though I'd barely seen this pitcher in nearly a week. But he has just an incredible amount of charm. He told me that there were at least eight guys on his club who wanted to go to bed with *me,* even though there were a lot of other girls around the team hotel.

I finally got loaded enough so that I felt I could do it with this "gobbler." But let's put it this way; it was such a sobering experience that no matter how drunk you were, it still would have been sobering.

There were about fifteen people in the room while I was being gobbled. All were baseball people, because I wouldn't allow any girls to come in. I was so uptight, I wouldn't even take my clothes off.

I was a little apprehensive; I thought if one of those guys was drunk enough, he might just hop right on top of me and they could all fuck me right there and I'd be out of luck, and I didn't want that to happen. Maybe that was being naive. I mean, I was doing something that was naturally going to turn on a few men. But most of those guys were so loaded by that point, I guess I didn't see them being sexually responsive. I didn't get undressed, though. Just pulled up my skirt. It was summer anyway, you know, and I don't wear underpants in the heat.

103 *maggie*

The guy who gobbled me wasn't drunk. He kept talking to me, reassuring me, telling me not to worry. I plugged my ears and closed my eyes.

I tried my damndest not to come. I wasn't going to give anybody any satisfaction. But I did come, and it really showed. After a few minutes—five or ten, I can't remember—I just really came. It must have showed all over my face. Sometimes I get noisy when I come, but in this case I held it in. Still, my coming showed: my hands grabbed, my toes curled. But most of the time while it was going on, I was really being a bitch, because I didn't want to do it. But I did.

When it was over, one of the players really put the capper on it. He said, and he was kind of disgusted, "I guess now you're one of the boys, huh?" It was just symbolic of, yes, if that's what I had to do to be one of the boys, then I was.

And another player said to me later that he was sorry he didn't help stop the gobbling. He said he saw that my eyes were pleading. But nobody made a move to stop the thing. It was over quick enough, and I got up off the bed right away.

Then, a few minutes later, one of the players at the party said he didn't think I could get him hard. I'm competitive by nature. All anybody has to do is threaten me, and I'll jump right in. So I tried. But the player was so drunk, I couldn't do anything for him. I did try while the five or six guys still in the room watched. He was just too drunk, though. So everybody started leaving, except me and one player. And he invited me down to his room.

I wasn't sure what he wanted, but I was so loaded I just took off my clothes and got into his bed. Then I remembered that I didn't have any strawberry jam in my purse. I love to put strawberry jam on a cock and lick it off. That's when I'm not on a diet.

It all started a few months before when I was in bed with a player and got hungry for a strawberry sundae. That guy went down to the restaurant and came back with no sundae, just strawberry jam. But I was so hungry that I just smeared it on him and licked it off. It was fantastic. Gives your mouth much more saliva and much less friction. You know, you can get dry and your mouth can't slide as easily on a cock.

So on the night of the gobbling, I got dressed again and went down to get a jar of jam out of my room. Somehow, *another* player was *in* my room waiting for me, and I got rid of him as quickly as possible. I said, "Forget it tonight." And he passed out on my bed. He was still there when I came back the next morning.

I went back to the room of the guy I left the party with, and this is really embarrassing. I get great pleasure out of oral sex—giving it and getting it. And we were in bed, both smashed, and the player went down on me. That was the last thing I can remember; I passed out. When I woke the next morning and found myself in bed with this player, I had stars in my eyes. But he looked at me, and he was sobered up now, too, and said, "Nope." He was in a different frame of mind by then. Guess I really screwed up my one chance with him.

the stud's girl

(NOTE: One of my favorite baseball players was a light-hitting, third string catcher who survived for nearly five years in the major leagues on the strength of never talking too much. He was an extremely handsome bachelor who would walk around hatless on the field before game time. Attendant Bimbos would thus have no trouble spotting him. A teammate of his suggested the catcher was one of the game's most capable lovers. So one day I asked him if this were true. He wondered why I wondered, and I told him I was considering ghosting a book about sports sex if I could find an outstanding stud. He said I was wasting my time talking to him. He said I should talk to this bachelor left-handed pitcher from another club. This pitcher, the catcher said, really swung. This pitcher would be my best bet, he said. I thanked him and started walking away, assuming I had tapped his conversational resources for the next month. But a moment later he was at my side. "I just remembered," the catcher said. "That southpaw is okay, I guess, but there's this guy in the other league who's all by himself in the sex game. He's either married, or separated, or divorced by now, so I don't know if he'll talk to you. But, Christ, is he a stud. S-T-U-D. That's him. That's your guy. Forget anybody else. Okay?" A week later I wrote the Stud mentioning my interest in collaborating with him on a book. He never answered. Probably too busy. What did he need with me when he had Georgie?)

georgie... *twenty-seven years old but appears older...Short, dark, sultry with a soft, sensuous and sad voice, gray eyes...divorced mother of two small children...married initially because of pregnancy ...From a straight, hard-working, Old Country family ...Describes herself as "a very sensitive girl," and does seem to be just that...Was a social worker so deeply touched by the depression of her clients that she lost weight and quit. "I couldn't cope with the sadness," she*

says...Had an eighteen-month relationship with
baseball's ranking Super Stud of the past half-dozen
years. When that ended, she had an essentially non-
physical fling with a professional football player—the
only sports affair she won't discuss at length. And there
were one or two-night stands with visiting baseball
players. Their names were not important to her, she
says. Nor, in retrospect, were their bodies. For Georgie,
they were something to do; time-killing intimacies
...Lately, she's dated very little—athletes or anybody.
"Until I find a total man, someone who loves my
children," she says, "I don't allow myself to get hung
up."...

Athletes are attractive to me, as they are to a lot of women.
Their physique, their style, their manners, even the way they
dress. Everything about them makes them a little bit more
attractive. Most of them are very good-looking. On my part—
and I can't speak for my girlfriends—going out with athletes
was a matter of their physical attraction. It was a matter of
that and loneliness and wanting to be with somebody for a
night. Just wanting to be with somebody.

O

I guess he had a reputation as one of the great swingers in
major league baseball. Definitely one of the greats. Let's call
him Artie. I mean, he was an artist. He was a very soft-
spoken person and had this air of total confidence about him.
He just kind of leaned back and watched you closely and
listened to what you had to say, but he was always on top of
the conversation at all times.

He understood women. He had a vast experience with
them—very vast—and he bothered to get to know them and
to understand what made them tick, why they felt the way
they did about a lot of things. He was able to work around
women. Artie was always on top of the situation.

I think he had a couple of years of psychology or something. (Laughs.) He's very intelligent as far as handling women. Definitely.

Even though we went together for a long time, he always continued to operate. He had to be an operator; it's his nature. He always will be as long as he lives. There were a lot of things he would say that would make me look at him and smile. He knew that I knew he was giving me a line of B.S. But he continued to do it, and we would just smile at each other. Not that he was a sweet-talker. I can honestly say that as long as I knew him, he never, never gave me an abundance of compliments, like other men would do. Not at all. No sweet talk—he just knew how to handle a woman. Operating with women was just an every day routine with Artie.

He always had to play some kind of a role. He could remember every single line out of a lot of movies he'd seen. We'd be together sometimes and he'd start acting out entire movies. I don't know how many times I had to sit through "Bonnie and Clyde" without actually seeing it. His memory was unreal. He did every single part. He was a great actor. I don't think he ever needed baseball to be an operator. He could have been anything and operated with women. Definitely.

()

I met Artie in a baseball bar. I'd been over at a girlfriend's house, and she called her guy, also a ballplayer. He was drinking with a player from the visiting club, with Artie, and told her to bring me over to the bar. And that's what we did.

He was giving me so much egotistical bullshit when we first started talking that I didn't like him. He just came on too strong. I told him it wasn't necessary for him to go through all that B.S. Just be honest, I told him. Just speak truthfully. Then he kind of started to mellow off and be himself, and I liked him. Physically speaking, I really liked him. He was so tall and strong. I was definitely attracted to him.

Artie and I and my girlfriend and her guy went over to the players' motel, and pretty soon the other couple went to another bar and left us alone. I think that was something the two guys had planned. Artie asked if I'd like dinner, what did I want to order? I told him turkey. (Chuckles.) He didn't even bother to order it from room service. He just grabbed me and started trying to kiss me and everything. I told him I really did want to have dinner, but he didn't pay any attention to me and just proceeded to try and get what he was after. Finally, after about twenty minutes of this hassling, he ordered my dinner and we mellowed out talking.

After room service brought the food, another ballplayer knocked on the door and came in. (Chuckles.) Right away, Artie gets up and walks out of the bedroom for a minute. When he comes back, his fly is unzipped. I just got real furious because I thought he unzipped his pants to make the other ball player think he'd been to bed with me. Really. I was furious, and I told Artie so right in front of his friend. Artie got all upset and said the zipper broke by accident. (Chuckles.) You know, I was really on my guard. I was very negative to everything. But, uh, then it finally happened.

I don't know exactly when I arrived at the conclusion that I definitely wanted to go to bed with Artie that first night. But I did. And it was really strange, because that was the first time I ever slept with a guy on the first night I met him.

I remember saying to him, "I don't know whether I like you or not, but I do know that I want to go to bed with you." He was pretty shocked when I said that.

I stayed with him the entire three days his team was in town. Sleeping with him was enjoyable. Very enjoyable. And then he left, and I didn't see him until the next season— although he did ask for my phone number. He said he was going to play winter ball in South America and might want to call me and have me come down with him. But I wouldn't give him my phone number. I didn't want to be added to his little black book.

For a while, I didn't know if he was married or not. That first night I met him, I heard him telling another ballplayer that he was going through a divorce. I found out later that it was a lie, that he was still married. But at the time I thought the divorce stuff was the truth, because here he was talking about it in a casual conversation. Artie could operate.

()

I saw him a lot the next season. He'd been traded to the team in our town and got my phone number from my girlfriend's player. So Artie called and asked me to come to spring training camp with him. And I did. I left my children at home with some relatives and went to camp. For a few minutes after I decided to go, I felt a little guilty. (Laughs.) But just for a few minutes. I kind of justified myself and went down to be with Artie.

Artie was the second man I'd slept with since I got my divorce. But he was the best I'd ever had up to that time. Definitely. In fact, to this day, he's still been the best. Mainly, he was the first man I ever *experienced* sex with. You know: *totally.* Athletes haven't given me orgasms usually. But Artie *really* satisfied me. Spring training with him was great.

I know a lot of the ballplayers there at camp knew that Artie was married and that I was staying with him, but that was no problem because they all think alike about things like that. Because they all do it. And even if some guys thought it was wrong, that didn't bother me. I don't put too much value on what people who aren't my friends think. Anyway, some of the other players had girls there, too. And some wives were there, but if a player's wife went home he'd find another girl. A few times it entered my mind that maybe all of these carryings-on were sort of disgusting. But I *was* enjoying myself.

It was fun. It was just fun. It really was. For me, it was a change of monotony. My life had been rather kind of dull and monotonous, and so I enjoyed this. It was quite a change of pace.

And Artie always bought me things. As long as our relationship lasted, he would get me gifts. He'd buy me clothes and buy my children clothes. He bought me dinners, many dinners. A lot of times he would even cook dinner for me. Just a lot of things. I guess you could say I felt like a kept woman. But I didn't care. He was lonely, and I was lonely, and I didn't care. Like, at that time I really didn't know what I wanted, so I didn't care about being kept.

I knew he had Georgies in other cities. I cared about that, but I understood. Any girl who is around that kind of life, even the wives, know that their husbands go out on them. But they expect it. They don't want to hear about it; they don't want their husbands to come home and tell them stories, but they know it's happening. Yet, if I asked him, Artie would tell me the stories when he came back from a road trip. But only if I asked.

I guess I was vain in a way. I took these things of his out of town as light affairs, and I didn't feel like I was a light affair. I felt that as long as I was the only girl *here,* that was okay. But I wasn't. Toward the end of our relationship, he was going out with another girl that was here.

Artie and I had fought about something and broken up briefly, so this one night I went to a bar with a ballplayer from a visiting club and Artie spotted me. The next night he saw me with a player again and came up and told me he'd flown a girl in from out of town.

I said to him, "You didn't waste much time."

And he said, "Well, what did you expect? For me to spend a whole weekend alone?"

He asked me if I wanted to see him later that night after my date was over. I said I would if he got rid of the girl he'd brought into town. And twenty minutes later she was gone. I guess he passed her over to another guy on his team. About two o'clock in the morning she comes knocking on his hotel room door. She asked him what had gone on, because I guess he didn't exactly explain the whole thing to her. He finally did, and she started crying. Evidently she was a very nice girl.

It was very sad to me, but I thought it was the best thing that could have happened for the girl's sake. She was young and appeared nice and innocent—the kind that can be bullshitted very easily by an athlete. So it was good for her to find out what was what. Find out the truth. I know it was a hard way to find out and it was a shame. She went right back home on the plane, but I think she was lucky that this thing had happened.

()

Artie would tell me stories about some of his girls in other towns—girls and women who had some money and would take care of *him*. I don't know if you could call him a gigolo, but he was a smoothie. When it came to taking women to bed, to physical aspects, well, he was definitely endowed. Oh, I don't mean endowed like *that*. He was just good in bed, okay? I think most women who had a sexual experience with him felt the same way I do, so that women who were older and had money could be conned by him into giving him gifts of money and other things. He had no pride, but I say that jokingly because I did the same thing—I took from him.

But there was never much he really could take from me, except sex. That was the only thing I could give him. I didn't have anything else to give. Just myself.

Artie taught me a lot of new things, a lot of techniques of being a good lover. After him, nothing any guy did or wanted me to do surprised me. I mean, I probably surprised them. But they showed me nothing new. Artie had showed me everything, all the techniques. Especially oral sex.

I really don't think a person can just learn techniques and be a good lover. There has to be a feeling behind it. Definitely.

Some ballplayers I was with after him found a lot of enjoyment in a couple of the oral sex things I did, but I never enjoyed doing it for them. With the other athletes, it became more of a routine thing—just part of trying to satisfy somebody completely. With Artie, though, it was enjoyable for me, too. And it satisfied him so much. So that's why when I went out with other ballplayers after him—there were, I think, maybe about seven of them—I would try to satisfy them as much as I'd satisfied him. I like to keep people happy. I figure if I'm going to that extent, I might as well try to be good.

But I never was able to reach a climax with any of these other guys. Oh, maybe with one guy from I think it was, uh, either Boston or the Angels, I had some enjoyment. But that's because he was a very nice person. But with the other six, I got no pleasure. I just happened to end up spending a night with these guys after meeting them in a bar. I didn't go out looking for this kind of thing, it just sort of happened. It was just a momentary enjoyment.

()

One time Artie wanted to move in with me. We had been mostly doing our things at his hotel, and it was convenient for us there. But this one time he sort of proposed to me. At first he used to just joke about wanting to get divorced and marry me, but he would never get any kind of an opinion or answer from me. After some big fight between the two of us, he would say that he didn't want me out of his life. Once I had completely detached myself from him for a few weeks and made it clear to him that I didn't want to see him anymore. Then he came back from a road trip and said that he just really didn't love his wife and that he really loved me.

He said he cared about her and everything, but that he wanted me.

I just didn't want him living with me. It may sound funny, because I hear myself talking contradictory. I mean, I let myself get into a relationship with a married man and everything. I spent night at his place and let him spend a few nights at mine, but I wouldn't let him live with me. Some of my morals I stick to, and some of them I just forget about.

He told me about all his plans to get divorced and marry me. It just wasn't anything I wanted, though. I didn't see how I could believe him. There were times when I did, when I felt he showed he cared for me—when he did things that were beyond the call of duty for an average ballplayer having an affair, things done just really out of love. He *did* have a love for me, but it was just for the time being, for the season. So, I really couldn't ever believe that he truly loved me. It wasn't the kind of love I wanted. And pretty soon, I just kind of passed through this affair with Artie.

I came to know what I really wanted and needed in life, and he didn't fulfill those needs when I realized them. I needed a man that's secure within himself. Artie didn't qualify. I needed a responsible man, a guy who could give me security. And that definitely wasn't Artie. What he was for me was a fascination, and when I began finding myself and knowing what I wanted and what I didn't want, well, our relationship deteriorated. He was really a great help in making me arrive at these conclusions.

()

We broke up a couple of years ago, but he still calls. I won't get together with him, though. I talk to him—on the phone. But I guess there are times I miss him. I find myself reminiscing with girlfriends sometimes about some of the ballplayers we've been with, and there is enjoyment for me in the memories I have about Artie. There was never any monotony with him. He never could be predicted; always a different mood, so he always kept your mind working. Your mind working and your body busy.

Sex with him just couldn't be routine. It was a matter of endurance. Sometimes it became a little bit too much. (Laughs.) Like the time we were in bed in his hotel for forty-eight hours straight. Two consecutive days, with room service bringing in all our meals. That came right toward the end of one season. I guess he was (laughs) gathering up for the winter, storing up for the lull. It really fatigued me. I thought I was going to die.

There I was, totally wiped out, and he was ready to go out and get someone else. He just loved sex. I mean, some people enjoy it, but they don't need to go out and express themselves on *everybody* they meet. He was the type of guy that enjoyed doing that.

Like most ballplayers, I guess he was just very insecure. It's a very insecure life. From one minute to the next they can be traded or something can happen to end their careers. And they go from one strange town to another. They're lonely, and they're insecure. It's the whole case of life.

And I guess that Artie was so good in bed that he made *me* a little insecure. A lot of times when we'd finish up, I'd feel inadequate. I think any woman except for a nymphomaniac would feel inadequate in bed with Artie. He could satisfy a nymphomaniac. Definitely.

I try not to think about sex with him. I try hard, but sometimes I get these yearnings. So I play a lot of tennis. I run hard and whack the ball hard and try my best not to think about these desires. I try to forget about Artie.

fresh and innocent

kay... *twenty-four years old; five feet five inches tall, one hundred two pounds ... long, straight, light brown hair and off-gray eyes ... clearly a debutante type ... high school social studies teacher from an extremely prominent family in a large city in the Southeast ... has had physical relationships with two professional football players—a lineman and a quarterback—plus a professional surfer and a professional golfer ... spent only two weeks with the quarterback; lived several months with the lineman ... was single ... didn't hestitate to discuss her football involvement, but became extremely squeamish and rather frightened, actually, when pressed about the golfer ... she would not offer his name, except to suggest that he is very, very well-known in his field—so eminent, in fact, that "he would have both of us killed if he knew I was talking about him to you" ... parents know of her relationship with him and don't disapprove—"as long as nobody gets hurt" ... speculate if you wish on the golfer's identity, but don't ask me ... I don't know ... repeat, I don't know, and I've even forgotten Kay's real name ... I don't want to be killed....*

I met him at a local tournament through a mutual friend. I really didn't set out to meet him or any specific golfer. It's just that my uncle was on the board of directors of the club, so I always was spending a lot of time there—but playing tennis, not golf.

It was a practice day, and I was walking the course with a couple of friends when we spotted this one player. It's probably better if I just refer to him as Joe. After his practice round, everybody introduced everybody else, and we went into the clubhouse for a drink. We had a few drinks, and he asked me out to dinner that evening. We were to go with at least two other couples.

That day I was very nervous being with him. Very. I was just kind of awed that this was happening. It was hard for me to believe that, uh, Joe was sitting there next to me drinking a beer.

He drove me home, and I walked right into my living room and kind of collapsed on the rug and told my parents, "Joe just asked me out for dinner."

They thought it was rather cute, because they said they were going to a cocktail party with Joe that evening. They said that there was no way he would be taking me to dinner because he was expected at the cocktail party. I said, "We'll see." And I did go out to dinner with him, although he made a short appearance at the cocktail party and met me afterwards.

I honestly didn't think he had anything else in mind besides dinner, but I guess I was so excited I didn't give that much thought. We were in a group at dinner. There was always a group whenever I was with him.

I felt more comfortable as the evening went on; didn't find it hard talking to him about golf and other things. And after dinner, I went home.

On the course the next day, I watched him tee off. Funny thing is, a television crew saw me standing there and said they wanted to film me admiring him. Just as they began shooting, he walked over to me and said hello and started a conversation. That film never made the air, though. I walked the rest of the course with him. I always walk eighteen holes with him, usually along with this guy who's a close friend of his. And after every shot, Joe would walk with us.

I enjoyed being seen with him on the course because I knew people were always looking at us, wondering who I was, I guess. I'm constantly being thought of as his daughter, which is kind of *cute*. I, of course, never had this feeling. I'm much more intelligent than he is. He didn't recognize this, though, and I never made a point of telling him, although we have argued about political things and women's lib things. He thinks he wins all our arguments, and maybe he has.

We had dinner on the second night. Again with a large group. Always. He preferred it that way. He never had to tell me why, but I knew. I mean, he was married, and people recognize him, and it's just better for him to say that he's with a group.

It didn't bother me when we went out to dinner that way. But we didn't always go *out* to dinner. We'd eat in his hotel room sometimes. There are many times that I've been alone with him.

He took me back home again the second evening, but before the tournament was over I did end up spending the night with him. It was the last day, but to that point he had never said anything about it, and I'd had no tremendous interest in doing that anyway.

For the first couple of days, maybe it was an ego thing for me to be with him. But after that, I didn't want to be seen with him. Golfers are cool—they don't acknowledge anything, but other people had started talking; I started feeling strange. I didn't like that feeling. All that talk was reflecting on my parents and me. I mean, I actually heard people saying that I was Joe's girl at the tournament. Not that they were being critical really, but I didn't feel that I wanted to be that public, because our relationship had begun to become more of a private thing.

My parents were hearing the same talk, and one of them said to me, "If you're going to do this, would you mind asking him not to put his arm around you while the two of you are walking around the club?" It had just got to be too public. That's all there was to it.

I think he felt the same way. Putting his arm around me was just a casual thing. He tried to make the relationship very private, I think.

We had dinner alone on the last day. I'd walked the course with him again, and after his round he asked me to come up to his suite for dinner. And it seemed pretty natural to go with him. Not that I assumed how the evening would end, but we had talked about a lot of his personal things—and I don't mean just about sex. We talked about his marriage. He told me that it was very, very stable and that he loved his wife very much; that if I wanted him on those terms, okay. I obviously did.

We had dinner in his room. I can't say that what you call "the natural thing" followed. Not exactly. I don't feel I should talk to you about it.

I can't tell you how I felt about what exactly took place that night. I'd have to go into it too much, and I don't care to do that. I wasn't worried about what he might ask of me; he's not a demanding person. And I wasn't about to demand anything.

You're asking questions about something that may never have happened that night. I was there. That's all I can say is that I was there.

()

He left town when the tournament was over, but I expected to hear from him again. Not that he assured me he'd call or anything, but I just knew I would. He seemed to like me; we had a good time. And I did hear from him—a day later. And when he played an exhibition nearby, I joined him briefly.

Then two months later he asked me to come to a tournament with him. I think he cared about me. He paid all of my expenses, and I spent the entire tournament with him in the house he was using. I had a great time, complete V.I.P. treatment, even though every time we went out it was always with other people.

I've never felt that I was just one of his girls. There was a lot that happened that we're not going to get into, but I never had the feeling that I was just one of several along the tour. I've teased him about having girls in other places, but he'd deny it. I don't feel that anybody can *belong* to anybody, but he was extremely possessive of me, and extremely jealous. He knew about some other men I was dating at the time; apparently someone had told him. We did discuss it, and I'd say, "I don't ask you to give up things...people."

When we'd talk about the possibility of him taking other girls to other tournaments, he would say that he doesn't. I believe him when he says this, but I know differently. Too many people have told me too many different things.

We've been to three or four other tournaments together, and I've seen him at places other than tournaments.

He's really another person to me—not somebody I just read about in the papers or hear about on broadcasts. He wasn't a name. He was himself. He was Joe.

()

My physical experience was totally different with him than it had been with any other man. No, not better. Perhaps not as good as some others. I don't know if it was my fault or his. It just wasn't as good as some others.

I've thought about this, trying to figure out why it wasn't better. Perhaps because it was always something clandestine, instead of something that was open—something I could openly show. I think there's more to it when you can be open and loving without being afraid that someone is going to see you. This is more because of the fact that he's married than because he's an athlete. What I'm saying is that it would be the same with any married man.

I didn't feel any sense of guilt. But maybe—perhaps—what

I felt was a sense of fear and inhibition that it wasn't going to be good and that he'd say. "Oh, well, there's millions of other girls who...."

I know that I'm saying two different things: that I may have felt inhibited because he was married, but that I also was so worried about being too inhibited and not pleasing him, and then being discarded by him. Yet, I really don't know.

We're talking only physically, but there's so much more to it.

I like to please him. I want to please him because I really enjoy being with him. I don't want to lose him right now, though maybe it would be better if I did. Better for me. I guess I'm just developing an emotional attachment to him. It hangs me up a lot. When I should be doing something that I really want to do, I'm off tripping around with him. He's the only married man I've ever been involved with.

The physical aspect is not the basis for our relationship. The reason he said he liked me at first was because I was fresh and innocent. Sure, I feel I'm like that. But with him, I overly portray those qualities. He likes that. He likes my youth, my freshness, my innocence—and when I first met him, I wasn't putting on any pretenses. But later, I started playing the role just a little bit—perhaps emphasizing that part of me. But I think all of us can fit into a role for somebody. I can be comfortable doing that. You have to fit into what the situation demands, as long as you don't overdo it.

So I was being what he wanted me to be, but by the same token I was afraid I wasn't always pleasing him. And he would tell me when he was pleased with me. *Of course*. And he pleases me.

I wish we weren't talking about him. I'd much rather talk about football. I don't think this is something that I should be really doing, and I want to erase this whole tape.

You don't know who we're talking about, but I do, and it bothers me to be talking to a stranger about our relationship.

121   *kay*

I would like to drop him from our conversation right now. It's making me very uncomfortable, and I don't like to feel uncomfortable. I know he's much more interesting than football, but please let's drop him.

()

(NOTE: A few weeks later, I met a friend of Kay's, a gal who'd known Kay since college days. She knew I'd interviewed Kay for the book; she also was aware of Kay's relationship with "Joe," the apparent superstar professional golfer. The friend said she had spoken with Kay about "Joe" many times, and gave me her own thoughts about that relationship. Because the two women are such good friends, I didn't feel I'd be intruding on Kay's discretion by relating the friend's attitude. And so, here's Kay's friend on Kay and "Joe"....)

()

I think Kay's involvement with him is the most ridiculous thing I've ever heard of. Anybody who does that is kidding themselves. How can you imagine that that person could care? Even if that person says things to you? Things like: "Maybe someday it'll be just the two of us." It just never will be, and you know it. This person is established, so why bother going out with him?

I can't imagine that she believes something *will* happen someday. She can't be that stupid. I think it's just that she feels it's neat to be seen with someone like that. I think that's the whole thing for her. An ego thing. I know it would be for me.

If I were in her situation, I don't think I'd kid myself as much. But see, I don't know what the relationship is—as far as the intimacies or anything like that.

I know she cares about him, but I think she cares about
him ninety percent as a name and ten percent as a person.
She won't admit that to herself, though, and if I was in that
situation I wouldn't either. Nobody can. But still, it's hard
to judge somebody else's relationship. So, maybe I'm not
right.

She really enjoys herself with him. He's very nice. I mean,
he treats her so well. I think he really cares for her. But it's
nothing that would be serious. He thinks that she's a cute
girl; maybe he enjoys going to bed with her. I just don't
know.

There have been times when Kay and I were supposed to
meet him someplace, but we've never gone because it just
wouldn't be a neat thing to do. When somebody's in the
position he's in and is married, too, well, you just can't follow
them. You do get to be seen by people.

I know that she gets together with him sometimes when he
invites her. But she goes with caution—and always with a lot
of other people.

the married bimbo

pauline... *forty-nine years old; a tall, slender, leathery platinum blonde; housewife, mother of two, grandmother of three; married to the same man for twenty-five years, lives in a major city in the Southwest— within easy driving reach of several important golf tournaments...estimates she's had affairs with about twenty golfers, many top names then and now...only once did her husband learn of an indiscretion, but she managed to keep the marriage together...sex to her is "a God-given thing, not to be tampered with"...has introduced many girlfriends to golfers, on request of both the girls and the golfers...is at ease in almost any situation, a bearing corroborated by a friend (male), who says: "You wouldn't be ashamed to take her anywhere." ...She describes a pro tournament as an event in which "the days are long, but the nights are longer"...best example of tourney sex, she says, came from a girlfriend, who reported moments after the last golfer putted out on the last day: "Oh, I'm so glad this thing is over. I've had so many pricks stuck in me the last four days, I feel like a pincushion"...it's all that fresh air, says Pauline....*

I guess golfers are the only athletes who turn me on because I identify so much with the game and because I've played golf so much. I still love and thrill to a beautiful golf shot, whether it's a long shot off the tee or a good iron shot that's hit simon-pure and cleanly to a flagstick or a putt that curls into the cup. I think these all are exciting things. And then there are the colors of the golfers' clothes—the bright, lively, fashionable colors that every woman loves. You can identify;

you can feel a part of this whole atmosphere. It totally excites me.

And these gentlemen have such superb mannerisms, much poise on the green—something the young golfers should always try to observe in the older ones.

I really think you can feel more of an intimacy—and an empathy—with a pro golfer than any other athlete because you can get so close to him at a tournament. As far as I'm concerned, there are a lot of women—a lot—who come to a golf tournament not because they care about the game but just because they like to watch the golfers. That's why pro golf has become so big, really. The colors and the intimacy.

I can remember as a girl watching Ben Hogan win a big tournament. Years ago, of course. It was in those days when you could walk the fairways, before they roped you off. I was in Hogan's gallery, standing not far from his caddy, and I could hear Hogan, between puffs of his cigarette, asking the caddy in that sedate and reserved way of his, "Is it a seven iron?"

The caddy would approve, and Hogan would peer straight at him the way he always did and take one more drag and then hand the caddy the cigarette. He'd take that seven iron, make the shot and then get the cigarette back. That, I think, is poise personified. You could get a feeling for the game and the golfer just watching that. Not necessarily a sensuous feeling for Hogan, because he always seemed so mechanical, more than a mere human. But you could really get stirred up about golf, about the game. You watched this great seven-iron shot and knew you were standing right next to perfection.

In later years, I would see a golfer do something great like that and just know that I wanted to be with him.

()

There have been times—and it's great—of making love right out there on the golf course. You have to worry some about the little lizards that are crawling around on the grass, but it's great, it's fun.

During one tournament this golfer and I were walking around one evening; it was a warm night, and you don't have too many clothes on and you can get all keyed up. We were just walking and talking about the day's play, about that particular hole we were passing. We got to the green, and....

I guess every golfer wants to lay a girl on a golf green somewhere. And it happens. That night it happened on the twelfth or thirteenth hole, somewhere along the boondock area. It felt good—we didn't have a blanket and the green was slightly moist and damp and dewy, but it was just great. Like nature intended, I guess. It was very nice, quite delightful. Guess I've done that twice.

I remember once kidding a visiting Scottish golfer that we did some things over here that they didn't do there, that we American girls loved the natural things, too. And he said, "Suggest something."

"Like being laid in the bare grass on a green," I said.

He laughed and said, "Oh, we've done that, too."

And I said, "Oh, I guess that you're not different from us in the States then, are you?"

It's a cute thing, and I think there have been a lot of girls that get laid out on the golf courses. That green is so soft and velvety.

O

It's probably true that I can get stirred up sexually just watching a golfer I care about while he's playing. When he's swinging, he's got this hip and body motion that gets to me, this lateral shift. The golfer's pants fit tight; they're snug. You see this tight fit of the clothes; you see their buttocks; you see their body make the turn; you see the snugness as the backside comes in view as they finish the swing. And it does sort of turn you on. It does. Then you see their accomplishment—the ball going through the air—and it gets to your soul. You watch a golfer through all of this and you say to yourself, "Gee, this guy must really be good in bed." You want to think that.

I've never thought much about the clubs and the balls in golf being phallic symbols, but I'll tell you that the golfers do kid a lot about sex while they're playing. This one day while I was walking a fairway, a golfer says to me, "Oooh, I get a hard-on just looking at you."

I told him, "Look out, you can't swing a club with that thing in the way." He thought that was so cute.

They're great needlers, golfers. They'll needle each other about girlfriends, about fancy cars, about cigars, about missed putts. They have a lot of feeling for each other. I think they have a lot more feeling for each other than even women friends do.

O

I've always played discreetly, very discreetly, most discreetly. Many chances I've had I just didn't accept because of the fear of what possibly could happen. I think, why should I take a chance on a one-night stand. Although these gentlemen turn me on, many of them are around for only one or two nights and I might not possibly see them again for another year. If then. And it's not hard to tell which of them have just one-night stands in mind. You can always tell that.

But the close friendships I made with some golfers have lasted through the years. Most of the ones I've been with, I've been with repeatedly whenever they're around this area.

They always find a way to get information to me that they wish to see me, although they'd never call me at home. They'd always find a way to pass the word to me—either through a friend at a golf club or a confidant of theirs. And it usually works out really good.

127   *pauline*

When I have plans to get together with a gentleman, I just tell my husband that I'm going to a golf tournament. That's all. I don't attempt to make any other excuses. Sometimes it works out and sometimes it doesn't. And if I don't feel that I can work it out to get together with a golfer, then I don't—and the golfer is always most understanding. They never seem to let their ego get hurt or shattered if we can't get together. They understand.

I once had to break a date with a golfer so I could catch a flight home, so I left a note for him. Didn't see him until a year later, and he understood.

When it comes to out-of-town tournaments, I always tell my husband that I'm either going with a girlfriend or that I'm going to meet a girlfriend there. And a number of times that's what I really do.

My husband is quite accepting. I tell him I'm going, and he doesn't pursue it beyond that. In fact, he has come to some tournaments himself, and at least a couple of times I have introduced him to pros who were my friends. He, of course, knows most of them from their pictures in the papers, and a few he's met on his own.

But except for that one occasion, years ago, I've never been caught. Hope I'm not living on borrowed time. Maybe it'll all cave in at once. Hope not. That would be dreadful.

()

I had the chance to marry two of the golfers I spent some time with. There would have been divorces, and then we would have married. But I considered the angle of all that traveling. I do love traveling, but I don't think I could travel at the rate they do, at the pace they do. You know, sometimes having to qualify on a Monday morning and then taking a couple of days to get organized at a tournament and then having the frustration and anguish of maybe not making the cut. It's a tough life for those boys, and maybe that's why I have so much sympathy for them and my heart goes out to them. But of course it isn't just through sympathy that I enjoy seeing them.

I know I love the game and the atmosphere, but I couldn't take the golfer's pace on a regular basis. And I think it does get tiresome to most of the wives. It just gets to be a pretty bad hassle for them, that's why so few of them stay on it.

The way I've got it now is really just fine for me. I've got the security of a home and family, yet there's enough golf action that I can play when I want to, be with a golfer pretty much when I want to, add the variety and spice that golf seems to give me.

Some people say there's never a dull moment in my life. Well, yes, there are plenty of dull moments. However, I do treasure my time with the golfers. And it isn't just an ego thing, it isn't just being with them because they're celebrities. I've had occasions to go out with celebrities from other fields, too, and they just don't turn me on. Not even actors.

Maybe it's just because I think golfers are good sex partners. That could be it. They're much stronger sexually than other men I've known. Golfers are perfectionists in their game and they're perfectionists in their sex. They're physical people; they must be, because golf is such a tremendously physical sport.

And most of them have about the same kind of sexual technique. They have this gentlemanly, tender feeling toward a woman. This tenderness always shows. And in preparation for the sex, they have a lot of class: they wine and dine you with courtesy and gentleness. It's just a beautifully polished way of living.

When you finish all this lovely entertaining, they just say, "Gee, let's go make love." That's a great invitation instead of just saying "Let's go jump in the sack and get it on and off." That's a crude way of putting it. The golfers know that their soft terms will melt a lady.

They like their foreplay in bed; it's a proper prelude to making love. They do enjoy the foreplay. And they're always so clean; they're very concerned about keeping their bodies clean. If they've just finished a round, they'll first jump right into the shower. I've been invited to many a shower, and that's fun—showering with them. Couple times I've made love in the shower—times when the fellows would get so excited that they couldn't wait to get into bed or if it had been a long time between visits. I remember one time that was really something: making love in the shower then going skinny dipping outside in the swimming pool. It was fabulous. We were in this enclosed villa, and it was really living.

They seem to like to get their clothes off in a hurry and relax that way. I've kidded them about being nudists, but this all is foreplay, all keyed to being a tremendous build-up for having sex.

They enjoy tremendous climaxes. Tremendous. And of course I do too. I climax easily. Yes. Yes. Their fine techniques just get me all keyed up. I have to say that they're just great. And I must say that I've found the same to be true with the top players—the top money winners—as with some of the young men who are new on the tour.

O

Only once have I ever experienced a problem in bed with a professional golfer. Only once; it was something I'll never forget. It was with a young man, and I guess it must have been an ego thing with him. He felt he wasn't built sexually like he wanted to be. Like the men say: he wasn't hung well. So he brings out a dildo.

I said, "Where in the world did you find *that* thing?" I wouldn't let him use it on me. Absolutely wouldn't.

He said, "All the girls like me to use this with them." And I just couldn't believe it. Just couldn't believe it. I told him to put it away, and we went ahead without it. I was satisfied.

O

I'm not loose with my morals. It's just that some men turn
me on. That's all. I hang on to the old Victorian principle of
never playing around in my own house. I just sanctify my
house in that respect. I've been in my own home alone with
golfers I have feelings for, gentlemen I've had involvements
with, but I never let anything happen there. A couple of
times a golfer has tried to get something going when he was
at my place, but I've always said to them, "This is not a
playground. This is just not it."

I wouldn't have been comfortable doing anything in my
own house. I don't know if that feeling justifies my other
actions, but I do have my own code of morality, and with me
comfort is the thing. I have to be able to move comfortably in
my own area.

And the golfers themselves have to be comfortable and
discreet. We can't be seen alone too much, and if we do want
to go to dinner by ourselves we just have to seek out an
insignificant place where the golfer won't be recognized. Or,
we'll often just have dinner in the room.

Still, I continue to play because of my affection for the
game and for the men. I suppose I may just be the kind of
woman who needs more than one man. That's not unusual.
But again, I can often be content with just one man. I know
that there have been times when I've been called by a golfer
and I've told him to forget it, that I wanted to spend the
evening with my husband. I'll just say, "I can't make it
tonight. I'm staying home with my husband."

I just can't put my finger on it. All I know is that there are
certain things that charge you up, and it has nothing to do
with any lack of a physical relationship at home, because
there is no lack. And this is even true of a few of my
girlfriends who I've fixed up with golfers. They stay married,
but these golfers just somehow charge them up over a long
period of time. There's nothing wrong with that. People are
people. Pro golfers may be big celebrities but they have a

deep-down emotional quality; they're downright human; they're just regular, God-created people, They've been given a special talent, sure, but that's part of life, part of people.

()

Most of the golfers I've gone with have been married, but one long involvement was with a pro who was single when I met him. The first time I saw him, he asked me to go to dinner with him. I said, "Don't be ridiculous. I'm older than you are."

He said, "That doesn't matter. What's a couple of years? Anyway, I like girls older than I am."

I said, "But I'm married."

He said, "That won't matter."

I said, "Maybe it doesn't to you, but it does to me." And I didn't join him for dinner, even though I was quite attracted to him just watching him on the course. I guess I turned him down because I felt that he was shopping for a mate. Guess I've always felt it's safer for me to be with the married golfers, that they couldn't lose any more than I could if we got involved.

I had dinner that night with a group of other golfers, and while we were finishing the single guy comes up to our table and tells me what his room number was. Very embarrassing. Very.

With me at this tournament was a girlfriend who was quite big and buxom, so I used her to pull a trick on the single guy. The two of us girls went to his room, and the door was ajar. I pushed it open and said, "Hi, honey, I'm here," and walked in.

He was all bedded down for the night, and he said, "C'mon, jump in." With that, I gave my buxom friend a push, and she landed spread eagle right on the bed and just about squashed him. He let out one scream, and she did too. Both at the same time. Their screams were heard all the way down the hall, while I'm standing at the doorway laughing. My girlfriend got up right away and ran out of the room so he wouldn't recognize her. And I beat it right out to my car figuring the guy would never forgive me for that joke.

Saw him on the course the next day. He came over toward me with a driver in his hand. I said, "You're not going to hit me with that, are you?"

He said, "That was pretty cute. The fellows are still razzing me." He thought it was a funny little trick. He understood. And that shows what a great guy he was. We ended up having a very nice relationship together over the years. We became very, very good friends.

During one tournament we went to church together. He was going to confession and asked me to come. While he went into the booth, I just waited in the back of the church. I decided not to go into a booth myself. When he finished, he came to get me and asked why I hadn't gone to confession myself.

I said, "I wouldn't dare go. If I stepped in that confessional, I'd probably explode it from everything I'd have to say."

Didn't go to bed with him that night either. I didn't want to break his confessional. We laughed about it.

()

I guess I feel guilty sometimes about my affairs with these golf gentlemen. I guess everybody feels guilt, and you feel some remorse. But then you wonder, well, it's pretty good to be involved with somebody like this, to care about them even when you're just walking the course with them and not having sex. I've had that same feeling of caring with quite a few of them. It has to be something quite deeper than just sex. And I don't feel I have to justify these feelings, because I do think I have a good marriage. I really do. I don't think I'd want to end my marriage, and I have had several chances to. But I never have.

133   *pauline*

I guess it's like any other marriage; it has its ups and downs. But most of the time I've had a great deal of freedom in my marriage. I don't think I could stay in a situation if I didn't have freedom. I know that my husband has a lot of freedom also. But if we were to tie each other down, it would be like birds that couldn't fly. I don't think any person has the right to do that to the other. Not that we're all free souls or free spirits or libertines in any sense of the word. But let me put it this way: I think the young people now have the right idea when they just go and take up residence with each other. I approve of that. They say this new thing of living together might destroy the institution of marriage, but I don't think so.

Those of us who have stayed married have had our sufferences and burdens to bear. But it's the same thing with these young people who just live together. They'll have burdens too. All I hope they do is show a responsibility to any children they might have.

I don't think I have the right to tell my husband what he can and can't do. I think we both have the right to use the minds that God gave us. Maybe I sound addled; maybe I sound as if I've deviated from certain principles. But I don't think so. We all can't do everything by the accepted form. All we can do is try to stay within the right precepts as we see them. I mean, my girlfriends would never infringe on my rights if they knew I was definitely serious about some golfer. And I wouldn't infringe on them either—even though I've had a few men who date my girlfriends call *me*. So there is a line you draw. I don't know if you'd call it a certain kind of personal honesty, or a moral code, or what.

You just try to set up your own principles and stick to them. I don't care if the man next door doesn't approve of me. I wouldn't tell him how to run his life, so why should he be able to judge mine? I want my freedoms, and I don't abuse them within certain limits. I guess if I didn't have this freedom, I wouldn't have stayed married.

My husband takes time off alone just as I do. And I don't know what he might be doing when he's away, or when I'm off at a golf tournament. I care about him, but I wouldn't make myself a nervous wreck worrying about what he might be doing. I did call him from out of town once early in the morning but couldn't reach him, and I worried about it. I guess he just didn't hear the phone, because he's a sound sleeper. I have to believe that he was just sleeping soundly that night. Whether he was out gallivanting around that night is his business, it's on *his* soul. That's the way I have to look at it. The same way that what I do is on my soul; I have to answer for that, for all my sins—as multitudinous as they might be. (Smiles.)

()

I've never seen any sex orgy things among the pro golfers, but I know they go on among the amateurs. I remember we were all drinking in a hotel room at one amateur tournament, and somebody asked me to go to a room across the hall to get some ice. When I opened the door, there were five or six nude bodies all sprawled around that room. They asked me to join them, and I said, "No thank you, all I want is some ice."

When I got back to my own party I told the people there what was going on in that other room. One of the men told me not to bother about that orgy, that we'd soon start one of our own. So I left. I don't go for these big, massive, free-for-all parties. The pros aren't like that. If they have a party like that, there's seldom more than four people involved—just two couples, two and two. I think only once have I had two pros at the same time. You know, making love at the same time.

These two pros were very, very good buddies and I felt that if it was okay with them, it's all right with me. The three of us had been drinking a lot, and we just went up to a room together and made love, made sex. That was about all there was to it. The drinking had keyed us all up sexually—drink has a way of doing that, but one of the fellows had so much to drink that he had a pretty rough time getting it off. He had an erection; he just couldn't climax.

The three of us were in one bed, with both of them fondling me; kind of a paradise for me. The one who'd really had too much to drink started on me first. For a while he was so proud that he was holding off, but then he realized that he wasn't going to make it. I'd climaxed by that time anyway. So the second golfer started. After that, we all went to dinner, finished and went back up to the room. I mean, only the fellow who didn't make it earlier and I went back to the room. The other golfer just excused himself. Once the first man had eaten, we got it together. It was just normal then, very much fun. I think the food settled him down, took away the numbing effect of all that alcohol.

I think that one of the latest things going around is nude parties. A couple of pros invited me to one just recently, but I can't go that route. I prefer privacy.

There was this one incident, though, when a girlfriend and I were with two golfers—whom I'm sure you would know—in one room. Each couple had their own bed. Whether they did much messing around during the night, I don't know. But my golfer and I sure did. When I talked to my girlfriend the next morning and compared notes, she said that they'd heard us, but that it didn't matter, that they got started later. I didn't know what had happened with them, because we stayed under the covers. We'd been drinking and I guess we all decided to do that just once. It was one of those things.

Another time, a man friend of mine was staying with a famous pro golfer at a tournament. The golfer wouldn't leave the room and we had to work around him. So we locked the door and made love on the bathroom floor. The floor was carpeted at least. Had a sore back the next day, but it seemed to be very enjoyable. The next evening, the other golfer again wouldn't leave the room. So I told my fellow to slip him a couple of sleeping tablets, then we could have an undisturbed night. (Laughs.) The man thought I was giving him cold pills. If he'd been drinking, I wouldn't have given him anything. But he hadn't been and wanted something for his cold. He said, "I haven't been able to sleep for a couple of nights with this darned cold."

I got this cute idea about the sleeping pills and told him they'd be good for his cold. But I didn't think they were going to knock him out like that. They sure did.

()

Some things just don't go with some galleries. Recently these two golfers were filming a match, and there were a lot of fans watching them. One golfer asked the other—quite loud—"Do you cheat on your wife?" And the gentlemen said no, he didn't.

The first golfer told him, "Well, neither do I. I just lay there and let the girls do all the cheating."

Several people just walked right out of the gallery. They thought that was such a sneery way of talking. I guess he was just trying to be funny, but sometimes in a mixed crowd people don't appreciate that kind of humor.

You can only kid about sexual things in a certain way on the course. A couple of times when I've been close to a green I've heard a golfer say to another who's just missed a putt: "Well, if there'd been hair around that hole you wouldn't have missed it." And that's a man's way of expressing the fact that a golfer was careless in putting or just not paying attention. You know: "If you were screwing a girl, you wouldn't miss the hole. So how could you miss that little putt?" Just a friendly way of needling each other.

They'll kid each other about having bad rounds because they were with a woman the night before. Although there are two different schools of thought on that.

Some people have the sort of health food idea that sex provides a feeling of body release and that it's needed physically in order for your organs and enzymes and muscles and nerves to be in complete accord with each other—so that you'll be completely relaxed. Golf is supposed to be such a relaxed game.

But then there are those who think that too much sex or too much night life drains too much from a person's system.

One golfer in particular, though, told me that he always felt relaxed after having sex, that it released his tensions and was very necessary for the benefit of his game. Wherever he was, he would find girls—even at exhibitions in remote areas. Whatever was around, he'd find. Even had a girl with false teeth once at some faraway place. For him, it was like fate always providing the necessary thing.

()

Now that the fairways are roped off during a tournament, it's a lot harder for the gallery girls to make contact with a golfer. They have to catch them at the turn, or right after the round ends, or at some convenient time. But believe me, the golfers will spot these girls anyway. They don't miss anything while they're out on the course. Often, the gallery girl just has to be standing in the right place at the right time, and the golfer will come up and say, "Hi." And the conversation will start. If the girl's nicely dressed, she'll probably get an invitation to drinks or dinner—and then it goes from there.

The society matron has more access to the golfers, though. Generally, she's a girl who plays golf. She can rather easily get involved by just being there in the clubhouse or cocktail lounge and making a comment to the golfer about something that happened during his round. If she knows golf, she'll say something like: "That was a tremendous shot you made on that par three," or "Congratulations on that fine birdie," and that strikes up a conversation, gets it moving along toward a discussion of dinner plans. I've seen this happen many times. But the girls have to be as discreet as the golfers in these things. Couple of girls I know weren't careful enough and reached the verge of divorce. One girl I know has been hung up on this same golfer for years, even after her husband found out about them. But this golfer still turns her on. She just sees him from a distance and she melts. It happens.

O

I've heard people say that women don't get as horny as men. But don't believe it. I know in myself that there are times I really *need* sex. In fact, I have several girlfriends who often call me up and say, "I'm so horny, I just don't know what I'm going to do with myself." I tease them about it, and tell them to go and take a cold douche—which is one way that a girl can do it, frankly speaking, whereas a fellow can't really do that.

It's just really tough for a guy to be going through mental pressures on the golf tour and then have to go through sexual pressures, too. I've heard of one or two pros who call their wives on the phone and will be talking to them and have an orgasm right there, thousands of miles away maybe.

Most men just feel they need to have their sexual release. It may only be once or twice a week, but they know that every so often they've got to recharge their batteries out on the tour.

I remember once having lunch in a clubhouse—like at noon time—and this pro came up to me and said, "Okay, baby, how's about going for a quick nine?" And I was shocked, because he was a man who dominated the game for years. I don't like that kind of advance, especially in broad daylight. But it just goes to show, that pros need that sort of sexual release anytime of the night or day. Anytime that they're turned on.

Maybe I'm kind of funny. I can do without sex at times. I can turn it on or turn it off. I have turned it off the moment I think a man isn't clean, or has a slight body odor about him. Still, I do wonder sometimes if I might be oversexed. I remember once looking over some of this pornographic literature that came from Denmark or someplace; looked at it with a girlfriend, and I said, "My gosh, this doesn't look any different than what we've been doing right along."

Went to see "Deep Throat" and told my friend, "I don't see what they're all excited about." I think it's wrong that they're putting it on the screen. I think this is something that should be between two people and should be confined to the four walls of a bedroom—whether you have mirrors on your ceiling to recharge you and really turn you on is your business. I don't consider anything sick about that. If that's what it takes to have a sexual release, fine. As long as it remains a private thing.

I once had a close friend tell me that after he and his wife have sex, she has to go into the bathroom and run warm, tepid water over herself—and that's the way she has a final climax. Seems a shame that she can't have an orgasm with the tool that God has given her husband. It must leave her husband a little bit frustrated. Has to. It's sad, and I feel sorry for her that she has to finish this beautiful act of making love by doing that in the bathroom.

And I also feel sorry for the wife who will say to her husband, "Okay, hurry up and get that thing in there and then get it out." There can't be much enjoyment to making love like that. There just can't be.

I was aboard a beautiful yacht once, and one evening we all kind of paired off in our cabins. After a while, I walked back up on deck and saw this dazed lady just sitting stark nude in the moonlight and clinging to a long, long cigarette holder. She and I looked at each other—I'd already gotten dressed—and neither of us pretended there was anything out of the ordinary. She said she'd already been to the captain's cabin, and calmly took a big drag on her cigarette holder. And that's the way I guess a lot of girls take sex—just as calm as ever. But I take it quite seriously. Quite seriously. I really do.

()

I don't think golfers hustle women all that much. I think they just want to get acquainted; they're just dying to tell someone how good their game was or how bad it was that day. I think they want to hear encouragement from someone else. That's all.

There was this one time I was working at a tournament and I had a couple of hours before I had to check in, so I was out on the course just watching. Jackie Burke was playing—and I don't think I talked to him before or since that day—and I told him, "Gee, you have a beautiful golf swing."

He said, "Would you do me a favor and gallery for me? Follow me please?"

And I did, and he birdied four holes. I was so thrilled. Told him, "I have to leave you now." Just like that. He didn't know me and I didn't know him. What a beautiful guy. They just need encouragement. It's an ego thing with them as much as with the people who watch them sometimes.

You know, too, I think this ego thing they have about their game is probably transferred into lovemaking. I've often found that to be true. Very true. They want to satisfy the woman and themselves, but I think that to them satisfying the woman comes first. A few of them have told me, "It's my pleasure to spoil you." It boils down to their striving for perfection, because that's the kind of game golf is. Wasn't it Mike Souchak—and he played football, too—who said that golf takes more out of you than football? Mentally, and possibly physically, too. He was right.

It's a sport they play alone. If they make an error, they blame themselves. If they lose, they lose on their own; they can't blame a team for it. And the same with lovemaking, and with meeting a girl.

141   *pauline*

They've always liked girls who are well-groomed. This is the kind of girl they marry, even though there are so many different types of girls available to them. You know, the society matrons, the gallery girls, the sports fans. The golfers have all these women categorized, and I've always tried to figure where I fit. But I just can't categorize myself, although I come as close to being a sports fan type as much as anything.

There are times I've gone a long distance just to see a tournament without trying to find a bed partner. I'd have dinner dates maybe, or go to a party, but no sex. I'd go only for the game itself, for the atmosphere, for the feeling of actually being there, being on the spot, being with *them*.

()

I met at least one wife of a golfer who I was involved with. Saw this one wife several times, in fact. I liked her. Actually, she seemed real thrilled that I remembered her name the second time we met. She made the comment to her husband, "Oh, she even knew my name."

I guess to her it was really something that maybe I recognized her for herself instead of through her husband— because he was a celebrity, you know. She had no reason whatever to be suspicious of me, and of course I did play it cool. I just kind of stayed out of their way, made no advances toward him. He brought her over to me; I didn't walk up to them. And this is the thing that the fellows on tour have to be very careful about. Because the girls who know the golfers can never be sure when the wives are going to be around in the gallery. So just a little thing like walking up to a golfer and shaking his hand can bring an irate comment from a wife.

There was this one swinger—golfer—on the tour who finally got married. His wife didn't travel with him all that much. He came home from a tournament one day and found her swimming in the pool and said to her, "Why didn't you come and gallery for me today? The tournament was so close to here."

She said, "Why should I go watch you play and watch all those girls making a fuss over you? I can't take all that mush stuff."

He became so mad that he threw his golf shoes into the pool at her. I guess this is just one of those things that wives of celebrities have: they can't take all that female adulation that their men get. I don't know whether it's jealousy or whether they just feel that they won't suffer if they don't see it. But then I've seen some wives who are so jealous that they follow their husbands all over on the tour—just never let them out of their sight.

I remember when I was seeing this single golfer friend of mine, we would avoid places where we knew this particular golfer and his wife would be. This wife gossiped a lot. She would tell other wives what she saw their husbands doing on the tour. Her reputation for being a tattler was a well-known thing. The single golfer just wanted to avoid her for my protection, not his. She became pretty unpopular. In fact, I think they later got a divorce. Would have been funny if her husband had been playing around, too. But I don't know if he did.

()

I don't consider myself beautiful, and yet so many pro golfers have sought me out, wanted to be with me.

I remember talking one night with a very, very well-known golfer about financial matters; somehow we'd got to talking about stocks and bonds, about making extra money, and he was a big winner on the tour that year. I suggested that Control Data was a good stock to buy at that moment, and the golfer just reared back and looked at me and said, "I didn't know that you had a brain." I told him to look into that stock, to buy some, that it had gone up a lot and would continue to go up. Sure enough, it did.

Listen, I know I'm not the college sweetheart, wholesome All-American-girl type that these gentlemen marry. But they do want to be with me, and maybe it's because of how I am with them physically. I give them pleasure. I adore giving them pleasure, I really do, and I guess these friendships wouldn't have weathered the years if I didn't give them this physical pleasure. Heck, there even have been times when I'll give them a rubdown if there aren't any of those kind of facilities at a club. If they ask me, I'll do it for them. Why not? They enjoy it.

()

I do try to think ahead about this kind of life, the way it has been for all these years. And I look at it like this: One of the top pros was going to retire, and I told him, "Look at the hearts you're going to break. How can you think of retiring?"

He said, "Well, I have to. The legs are going. It gets to be a chore to be out there on the course working."

I said, "You don't work for a living. You play for a living. When *we* talk about it, it's going out to *play* golf."

He said, "It's play when you don't have to earn. But when you have to earn at it, it becomes work. I just know that one of these days I'm going to have to retire."

And I repeated to him that he was going to break a lot of hearts. I said, "I'm even thinking about the day when *I'm* going to have to retire."

He said, "I'm going to tell you the same thing then: think of the hearts you're going to break. Fellows really look forward to seeing you."

I told him that I didn't realize that. I said, "I know that you fellows must do a lot of talking among yourselves about the girls on tour."

He said, "Well, we don't disclose too much, but I guess there is a little bit of this camaraderie—passing around stories about girls."

And that concerned me for a while. There was this pro who had a drinking problem—I was very sympathetic to it—and he came up to me one day and said, "Oh, I heard that you were one of the greatest gals that so-and-so had ever been with." He mentioned this other golfer's name, and he was a top golfer. I just cringed. But I knew that these two fellows were best friends. I was embarrassed, but I just ignored what the golfer said and walked away from him.

But that incident did put a thought in my head, because somebody might have overheard the man. I figured I better be careful, because if anything like that gets back to my home area it might be pretty dangerous. I cooled it a little bit after that.

I figured it wasn't worth destroying my future and my security. We all need this security in life. Without it, life is empty.

We all try to work so we can earn security for our later years. I think we can grow old gracefully but still have sex. There's nothing wrong with continuing to have sex. I had this old uncle tell me once that he was getting out of sorts with himself because he couldn't get it up anymore. And he was seventy years old. I was kind of shocked that he should say that to me, but it made me think: do you mean to tell me that I can have sex until I'm seventy? Oh, what a glorious thought!

I take care of myself. I try to eat the right kind of foods. I think you can stay oversexed for a long time but still be moderate. You can tame yourself to a certain level: get what you need, but take it easy. It would be like a person putting themselves on a partial diet. You have to make some sacrifices, deny yourself. And I have denied myself many times when it came to sex. I would have loved to have done a lot more things. Not that many more things, but a little more.

I remember one evening I made two visits to golfers and it wasn't out of the ordinary. Each of them was good sexually, and I seemed to enjoy it. Neither of them knew the other that well, and I didn't tell them I'd been with the other on the same night. I wouldn't talk. Never.

the little girl from plainfield

New Jersey, who made good by
sleeping with a receiver from
The National Football League,
although it wasn't in the program.

phyllis... *thirty years old, dark-haired, semi-
sophisticate scurrying through radio-TV advertising
world with great self-satisfaction and some success. Bit
chunky, but sportily handsome. Might pass for years as
a take-charge college sorority officer. "Life smart," she
says. Talkative, aggressive. Admits penchant for name-
dropping. Tennis freak who's never married. From
Plainfield, New Jersey: "Just a girl in a small town. It
could have been Pocatello. Most of my friends married
their high school or college boyfriends and came back
home and raised kids. But that wasn't for me. I would
have been stifled staying in Plainfield." Instead, dabbled
in broadcasting on both Coasts. Between things worked
in office of a National Football League team. Dated sons'
of two of the team's owners. And others.*

Before I started working for the N.F.L. team, the only
athlete I knew was feet. (Laughs.) I mean, I really didn't
know an athlete. I didn't know from football. I knew that
there were four downs and, you know, they went from one
end to the other end. But that was it. Just before training
camp opened that summer, this bachelor receiver comes into
the office and says, "I'm free for dinner tonight. Would you
like to go?" I told him sure, and that's how it started.

At the time, I had a boyfriend in Colorado, a guy I had
been going with for ten years, since our last year in grammar

school. But he was in the service. The Receiver didn't come on strong. I mean, if he had been ten other people coming on the same way, I probably would have accepted the dinner date. He was nice and it was a free dinner. He was a couple of years younger than me, but very sure of himself. Very pleasant guy, one of the nicest guys on the whole team.

None of the guys on the team ever came on strong to me, though. I'm not really the type that somebody comes on strong to. Probably because I'm more of a lady type. Unless I know someone, I'm reserved. I'm very friendly with people I know. I can fool around and, you know. . . . But until at least past the first meeting I would prefer not to have people think I'm too crazy, because I have a tendency to be kookie.

The Receiver and I went out a couple of times, although I had been warned that the girl in the office before me had been asked to, shall we say, vacate her desk because she had invited players to her home. But I never saw a memo on that or anything. I think that management was afraid we'd talk to players about salaries if we went out with them or became good friends. Isn't that terrific? I mean, can you imagine yourself cuddled up with a player you've wanted to get close to for six months, you're playing it cool and you're going to say: "I love you, and, by the way, that interior lineman is making thirty-eight thousand dollars plus a car and expenses." I mean, how ridiculous. I didn't even know how much anybody was making. Wouldn't have cared either. I just knew that I was making ninety-two-fifty a week, before taxes. Worst paying job I've ever had in my life. I guess they felt I should be paying them. This is show biz.

The Receiver was kind of confined to training camp after our first couple of dates. They had really strict hours there. I'd see him during the scrimmages sometimes. I think he had a girlfriend back home, and I had my boyfriend. He was just a rookie and impatient about getting a chance to play first string. I told him, "Listen, the regulars will get traded. Stick with the club. Just stick it out and you'll be fine." And I was right, eventually.

Both of us were dating lots of people. We just liked each other as friends. I probably treated him like another human being, and he never bullshitted me. He didn't have to impress me. We would talk on the phone, and I'd tell him things he did really well in the game or things he did poorly.

Our physical relationship was brief. Very brief. We had a date this one night, and he mentioned something about going to his apartment way down on the San Francisco Peninsula. He knew why we were going there. So did I. We didn't say it, but we knew. I had put on my brand new underwear. I mean, I really looked terrific. Just in case I was in an accident, you know, like your mother always tells you to wear clean underwear. So he picks me up at my apartment and we make the long drive down to his place.

This guy really did turn me on. You know, I would notice his rear end when he would run onto the field. I could tell him—without a number. He had the greatest behind of any guy I've ever seen in my life. I just thought he was really sexy. It wasn't even important that he was a football player. He could have been anything. When we got to his apartment, I was nervous as all get out. I had never been with anybody before. I was a virgin, and I was really nervous. I mean, imagine me, a punk kid from Plainfield, New Jersey, in bed with a guy from the N.F.L. And it wasn't even on the program. And we were in bed for about thirty seconds. He thought I laughed. Well, he must have been as insecure as I was because he jumped up and said, "Put your clothes on. I'm taking you home." He must have driven two hundred fifty miles that night—two round trips. And then he wouldn't talk to me for a month. I don't know why. I think he probably thought I was laughing at him, but I was terrified. So we didn't date for a while.

We went to bed together one other time. And then we both sort of giggled and laughed. (Giggles.) It was, I guess, like going to bed with your sister. I mean really, it just didn't work. So we laughed and he hugged me and stuff like that. He still called me every night. We'd talk about our other dates. We just really had a good time talking with each other. I'm easy to talk to, and I also listen. Maybe that's a fairly decent quality to have. But I'm very honest, and people know that I might hurt them when I say something. If somebody's my friend and they ask my opinion, they know they're going to get an honest answer from me.

I occasionally dated a couple of the single guys on the team, but there weren't that many of them. Then after I left the club, I sort of went out with one married guy. But not as a relationship. We're still friends today. I knew his wife and the kids and I've been over to the house and everything. But I was never really involved with him. Well, (laughs) just half involved.

One time we figured, well, why don't we do it? Why not? I was going to borrow a girlfriend's apartment, but she was out of town, and we were waiting for her to come back. We just drove around and around and around waiting for her. Finally it was time for him to go home, so we didn't do anything. He was really frustrated. I wasn't frustrated at all because I didn't know whether it was going to be good or bad.

Then later I saw him in another city. He was separated then. But that doesn't mean a damn thing: if he's married, he's married. I went to the team hotel trying to get two game tickets from him. I brought a model who lived next door with me. I was fixing her up with another one of the married guys on my old team. She was a very naive Southern girl. I'm sure at twenty-six she was still a virgin. Very lovely, and she didn't know diddly about football. She was into only being beautiful. The football player was really impressed because, like every model, she carried her composite pictures with her. So if there was a lull in the conversation, she would show her composite. And this turns guys on. I got good vibes from the player about her. He told me a year later that he really loved her, and he and his wife were very tight.

But, like I say, what these guys do when they are away from their wives has nothing to do with breaking up. If they do go to bed with somebody, it's just with a face. It has nothing to do with their family. It's like most men in business that you meet in a bar. You might go and shack up with them, have an affair, but you are not going to have anything to do with breaking up their families. They love their wives and children and everything. For whatever reason, they might be physically attracted to you; they might just need a little at the moment; they're not getting it for some reason. But whatever it is, you're not going to break up their home.

Anyway, like I was telling you, I wanted to get some game tickets from this old married player friend of mine. He was tied up at some sort of business meeting but told me to wait in his room. I went up there and knitted on a sweater I was making for another guy—and watched TV.

Finally, he came in. He game me the tickets and then he said, "Hey, you wanna?" And I'm going, "No, I can't." And I couldn't, and didn't. I was getting paranoid about a coach coming into the room and checking. I knew all the coaches and I didn't want them to think I was the kind of girl that would go into a man's room. But I couldn't mess around that day anyway. Big Red had visited. My friend was gentlemanly and understood.

My married friend is still very happily married. Let me emphasize that. He called me only today and re-iterated that he is very happily married.

0

My friend Lisa knew most of the Detroit Lions. She'd been dating one of them, a married guy. When they came to town she fixed me up with a Lion and we all went to their hotel. Some of the players had gotten a room for some girls. I just went in there to have a little champagne during the eleven o'clock bed check. They *had* to be in bed by eleven, literally, because the Lion coaches really checked. They might get up at one minute after eleven, but at eleven sharp they're in bed.

I sort of felt peculiar because Lisa had gone off with her friend someplace. There I am in a strange hotel without a penny in my pocket, without a car, no way to get back to my house. I was really ticked off. I was thinking about calling the manager of the hotel, who was the father of a fella I was dating. But that wouldn't have been too cool. Besides I couldn't say, "I don't know how to get home." I was twenty-six years old after all. And then Lisa calls me and tells me she's going to be with her player *all* night.

I said, "You're kidding. Where am I supposed to stay?"

She said, "You'll find a place."

One of the players pops into this room where us girls are. He was very, very nice and said, "Well come on, we'll go get a room for you."

I'm saying, "That's stupid. I don't even know you. You're not going to pay for a room for me."

And I look around and there's one girl passed out on the bed waiting for her friend to come back from bedcheck. I know when he comes back he'll crawl in the sack with her. I'm just sitting there, stone cold sober because I rarely drink much at all and never smoke. I didn't have a book to read or anything. And I'm going: "How do I get myself in these situations? How do I do it?"

I just couldn't think of any way to get home. I was even thinking about calling my boss, who didn't live too far away. But he would've gotten annoyed at me. And it's like eleven-thirty at night, and I couldn't impose on anybody. So I called the room of the Lion I started out the night with. His roommate was shacked up, he said, someplace else, so there was a free bed in his room.

He said, "All right, you can sleep here."

I walked around that big maze of a hotel there and I was almost in tears—like I was one of Pavlov's dogs. I started to cry cause I was just so ticked off that I was dumb enough to get myself into this situation. I finally found the Lion's dumb room. All he needed to do was to lay a hand on me and I would have clouted him into next week. I was not in a mood for messing around.

He sort of advanced toward me. He was half asleep, and I'm going: "Don't you dare." So he just did an about face and got into bed. I got into the other bed with all my clothes on, pulled up the blankets and just slept there all night long. It was just awful.

Next morning Lisa calls and asks me if I could help her smuggle her Lion back into his own room. I go to their room, and she's still in bed. I was throwing underwear at her. I had to go get her car, bring it over near their room and beep when it was all clear—when there were no players walking by on their way to breakfast.

Lisa's Lion finally gets on the floor of the car, and I'm driving him back to his room. It was ridiculous. All these black Lions are now walking by us on their way to breakfast and going, "Hi, what's happening?"

And I'm going, "Oh, nothing." It was like High School Harriet stuff, and here I am—twenty-six years old.

I'm going to myself: "I'll never let myself get into these dumb situations again. You deserve it if you're that stupid to come along like this."

It was just really childish. Not funny, just childish. It just seems to me that if somebody's going to do something, they ought to just do it. I mean, if Lisa's Lion was going to mess around with her, he ought to have been man enough to put on his clothes and walk out in the fresh air in the morning and go to his room.

That same night there was this incident involving a Lion linebacker. He met this very nice divorced lady at a bar. Not high class, I mean, you know, she wasn't me (giggles), but just a nice girl.

The linebacker brings her back to the hotel, although I don't think they were going to be shacking up or anything. She's in this room with me and the others during the bedcheck time—and right across the hall from us—who's there but a coach. So the linebacker comes to our room with two glasses and a bottle of champagne and goes to this nice girl, "Let's make a party."

She gets up and they walk to the door. A coach walks by, never breaking his stride, and says, "Nice girl. Five hundred dollars." And the linebacker got fined.

The coach didn't say, "Hey, don't go with her," or anything. Just "Nice girl. Five hundred dollars." And kept walking. I thought that was really funny. The linebacker just went "Awwww."

From what I'd heard, the guys on the Detroit team used to get fined left and right for messing around. But I think that's a problem that should have been taken care of at the coaching level. You know, the coach could have leveled with the guys and said, "Hey, this is the way it is." I think the guys would probably have not messed around as much. I don't know. Maybe that's not even for me to say, but it seemed like they weren't really treated like men; therefore they didn't have to act like men.

the in-laws were wonderful

diana... *twenty-four-year-old cocktail waitress from Southern California. Remarkable body. Wan complexion, long, lovely, red hair. Mother married four times, father seven. At time of interview had not heard from father in three years. Once left note on his door; he didn't respond. "If I were to die tomorrow, I wouldn't let him come to my funeral," she says. In younger days was deeply in love with dental student, who ultimately told her, "You're fat and ugly and nobody will have you." Lives fast, she says, but "that doesn't mean I'm hard." Paints. "I can relax only when I'm painting." she says. "I never even painted a happy picture in my life. Not even a clown." Slept with the first and second string quarterbacks of the same N.F.L. team. Major sports involvement, though, was living in the hotel room of a now-retired baseball player. She enunciated her guilt over the several months-long affair by writing a poem. She still keeps a copy, along with the small dog the player gave her.*

DIANA'S POEM

She held her head high
though the wound of
misjudgment was deep.

For you see, my friend,
the eagerness of society
was fast to condemn
the innocent, blameless and
unpremeditated love she held
for a married man.

155

So slow to learn,
so fast to forget
and so very eager to criticize
is society—toward the
almost forbidden emotion—
LOVE!

Dear God, please help those
who are so eager to condemn.
Help them to
observe
experience
and behold
the divine
universal emotion
love....

I was somewhat on the breakup with my boyfriend when I met the Player. I'd been in the hospital and I didn't want my friends to know I'd been sick. I was losing weight, down to about one hundred three pounds. I looked horrible. When I got out of the hospital, I stayed at my mother's house for about two weeks. Finally, she got very upset with me because I wasn't working and I wasn't going out or anything. She decided I should go out and have fun. She practically threw me out of the house. It was either I go out or go see a psychiatrist.

Then I went out and was sitting with a friend of mine at this bar. Some girl pointed to the next table and said that this ballplayer sitting there wanted to meet me. That's the kind of approach a lot of players use; expect you to be impressed that a message has come to you from a professional athlete. I don't particularly like that, so I wasn't being very nice. I just kept talking to this guy I came in with. And then another message comes over with a waitress from this ballplayer. I told her to tell him I'd be over in a minute. It was getting interesting because he was being so persistent. After about one more drink I went over to his table. By this time he had been drinking heavily. He was smashed. Creamed. I ended up telling him to go to hell and called him an egotistical bastard, something I very seldom say as I very seldom swear. I just got up from his table and went to stand over at the bar.

Why he wanted to see me, I'll never know, because I was so skinny and horrible looking. I saw him leaving and came up behind him and just kind of tagged him on the back. I told him I was sorry I was mean to him but that was just the way I felt. And I apologized. Both of us just kinda straightened up and started talking.

He finally said, "How would you like to go across the street for a drink?"

So I told him okay, but I left word with a couple of my friends to call me in about a half hour if I wasn't back, because I wasn't completely sure of him. And he was so big and he talked so gruffly. And I had never had anyone like that before.

We went across the street to the bar at the hotel where he was living and had a drink. Then he asked me to dinner, and I said okay.

"We'll have to go to my room for dinner," he said.

And I told him no, I wasn't going to his room.

"What did you say?" he said. He had such a strange, gruff way of saying things that I just immediately followed him up to his room. Honestly, he ordered every single thing on the menu. I never had anyone do that before, but I was so skinny he wanted to fatten me up. So anyway, we had this feast; I was like a little kid—you know, ice cream, steak, everything. It must have cost him fifty dollars. I don't know why he did it.

Afterwards we started drinking and were really just enjoying each other, sitting at a table talking about odds and ends. He decided it was time to go to bed, and I thought it was time for me to leave.

I'm very strange. I don't like to be touched. If I want to, I'll make the move. But I don't like a man to approach me. A man will never stop trying, so you just have to surrender when you're ready. I guess that's what I mean by making the move myself. Just surrendering.

Anyway, he was mad that I was leaving but he finally just said, "When you want me, let me know." It was five o'clock in the morning, and he walked me to my car and said a strange thing: "Diana, when I am through with you, you're going to be very strong physically and mentally both."

I thought that was very strange for him to say after just meeting each other. We talked for a while in the car, and I asked him if he was married. He admitted that he was: he didn't beat around the bush. And just the way he said it, I accepted it. I just right away didn't think anything of it.

We made a date for the next night, and the same thing happened. All the food, all the talking. I spent the night this time, and he made me take off my clothes and put on one of his shirts so I wouldn't get my clothes ruined. But nothing sexual happened. All of a sudden it was All-Star break, so he asked me to come over and stay with him for those three days. I packed a bag and did. And I guess this is when we first started living together, during an All-Star break, just about four or five days after I met him.

I told my mother what I was doing. She got highly upset about it. My mother has gone through four marriages and everything else, but to me she's always been a very kind woman. She's never gotten upset at me or anything else. But after I'd been living with my Player for a while, I went home one night when he was on the road and was sitting in my nightgown eating dinner. And my mother started talking to me in this nice voice. She goes: "Do you know what, Diana? You're worse than a prostitute. At least a prostitute gets paid for what she's doing. You're just a whore."

At that, I was simply shocked. My mother had never, never said anything out of line to me in her life or in my life. I got up and called a girlfriend and told her I had to get out of the house. I was crying hysterically, and left in my nightgown.

I said to my mother, "Well, if I'm a whore, I'm going out

and do my job." I tried to be just as bad as she said I was, and we didn't speak for a good five months after that.

I've had about a year now to think about why I moved in with my Player. I think he was a father image, really. I think that's exactly what it was. He was very easygoing until the minute I defied him. He'd turn into a blind rage immediately; he would come at me almost like he was going to kill me. And then he would think about it and just leave the room. I never had any discipline from any man. None at all. It was nice, and my Player was taking care of me. I could have been taken care of at home, sure, but he was just very nice. And there was never a total physical thing between us. We could go for weeks without it. That's why I say we were almost platonic friends, really. I mean, there were times he didn't want any sex and times I didn't want to.

He told me when I first moved in that I wasn't bound to sex with him, that he didn't want me just for sex. He said there would be nights I wouldn't want to, and that would be okay with him—fine, just tell him. He was very understanding about that. And during our relationship I wasn't getting any sex on the side either. He may have been. I'm not a domineering person at all; whatever you want to do, fine with me. Even if I find out about it, fine with me. I don't really care. Who am I to say anything? He's married. Really.

But I was that way with my dental student boyfriend, too. Once my Player called me from the road, from Philadelphia, and there was another woman's voice on the phone there. I always told him to go out, and then I caught him in the act. He tried to tell me the girl was his sister. All I did was laugh. I guess I believe in the double standard. You know, a man has to keep proving himself.

()

A team came to town that my guy used to play for, so we were sitting in a bar with a bunch of his old friends. And there was a man next to me with a sports jacket on who really impressed me. I would talk to him and I would cry. I just met him and I was crying and I felt ridiculous. My Player actually had to take me home. I couldn't stop crying.

I met the man formally the next day. He was a priest who knew a lot of ballplayers. The way he spoke and everything, it just got to me. I cried, I think, because he had such peace and serenity written all over him. The mellowness just got to me.

My Player just couldn't believe I was crying over this Catholic priest and went out and bought me roses. The priest himself told me that my Player wasn't in love with his wife and that the Player had told him he loved me. I guess the priest had known my guy and his family very, very well. And for the priest to tell me this, well.... He told me to do what I thought was right. He said that if I was happy, fine.

And while this priest was in town, my Player's in-laws arrived, too. It was his father-in-law with a new wife. I almost panicked when I saw them walking over toward us.

I said, "Do you think it's wise for me to talk to them?"

The priest was laughing. I was somewhat laughing, but I thought it was odd. The entire situation. He introduced me to the in-laws as his girl friend, Diana Darling. He always called me Diana Darling. And the in-laws never said a thing. Not at all. They treated me wonderfully. And they were very sweet. And I don't think the subject of my Player's wife ever came up. I mean, I never even knew the name of his wife. I knew he had two children at the time, but that was about all. I didn't want to know anything. That was his private life. I had this other part of him.

I learned from another friend once that my Player said he wanted to get divorced and marry me. I didn't want that. What would his wife and children do without him? That was his life. That was what I was thinking. I guess I would have been happy the rest of my life with him, but I wouldn't be that selfish to take a father away from his children. He loved his children very, very much. I'm not saying I'm a, what do you call it, martyr. I'm not really trying to be a martyr, just looking at it very realistically. I've gone through very many broken marriages and I know what it's like. I guess I identified with his children, and their father's love for them. You see, I never had a father's love. That was it, more or less. When the in-laws were in town, we all went to a cocktail lounge together for a little party. We had a round of Bloody Marys brought over every fifteen minutes. I loved those in-laws. They were nice, very nice to me. My Player told me I could relax, so I instinctively relaxed.

()

At the end of the season, when it was time for him to go back home, I told him I didn't want to see him anymore, that there was really nothing more to be gained from this relationship. I adored him, but if I was going to stay with him any longer I would be hurt. At this point, I had a barrier up. I would not let myself fall in love with him. The longer you are with someone, you go through too much together. I didn't want to go through the same thing I'd been through with my dental student.

So then it's spring training camp time again, and my Player called one of my girlfriends wondering why I hadn't come down there. He was upset that he couldn't find me and he was crying. He told her he wanted me back.

My girlfriend called me, and I called him. I really didn't know what to say, so I let him do the talking and he wanted me to come down to the training camp. But I wouldn't go. He called me every night for a week, three hours on the phone every night.

Then during training time, he had to come up to town for something. I met him, and that's when we started up the relationship again.

But when the season got going, he brought his wife with him. She was in an apartment in the suburbs. He was living with his wife, but I'd see him after every game and he called me every single day. After a game I would meet him at a bar near the ball park. We would usually just sit and talk. No sex really. That wasn't our big thing together. It was just a very, very close friendship, I guess you would call it. It was a very weird relationship. I know I was getting from him a fatherly type of thing. I'm not sure what he was getting from me. I don't know if he considered me his wife. I tried to be as understanding with him as possible. I tried to help him.

He used to say that he and his wife fought constantly, that they'd come to blows. I very, very seldom fought with him. I'm a very calm person, you know, so therefore he could raise hell or anything he wanted to and I would just sit back and listen.

For a while I thought that just everybody thought I must have been the biggest whore in the world. But I came to find out that nobody thought anything, really, about me. But nobody liked him. He was mean and gruff. He would fight any man that dared talk to me. You know, immediately. No hesitation. He would probably kill a guy. He was very, very possessive. But all the other ballplayers showed me respect. They were very nice to me about everything. Sometimes I would pick up their girlfriends they were flying in from out of town. A couple of married players' girlfriends. I guess I was the only person those players could trust.

I would meet these gals at the airport, entertain them for a couple hours, then take them to the ballpark. The players insisted that their girls come to the games. That's the big pride and joy for these men. My Player would get on me for not going to all the games. But I'm not a sports fan. I like baseball a little. I just go to the games to socialize with my friends. I wouldn't really watch the game unless I heard my Player's name announced. Then I would watch to see what he did.

He was traded early the next season. His wife went back home, and I went to live with him. He wanted me to go on some of the road trips with him, but I'm not really much for travel. I like to stay in one place. As long as there are things to eat and everything, I'm fine. I wasn't obsessed by him. I didn't have to see him constantly. He went back home to his family after that season ended, and I haven't seen him since.

He called me a few months ago from some minor league town at five o'clock in the morning. He said, "Diana Darling, don't worry. I'm gonna be back in the majors soon and I'll be out there." But then he retired and never called back.

the multi-media woman

sue ann... *twenty-nine years old; short, busty, cheery ("I keep my troubles within")... only daughter of a black contractor from Oklahoma... married at sixteen to an electronics engineer, but they seemed to quarrel every other month: "He would go home to my mother, and I would move in with his mother"... now divorced and raising two children, thirteen and ten years of age, on cosmetologist's salary... was a registered private duty practical nurse, but didn't like the night hours so switched to full-time work in a beauty shop and part-time usherette chores at a major league baseball stadium... dated seven ballplayers, all of them black, and slept with two... might have had sex with one of the other five, except "all he'd ever do when he came over to visit me was play baseball with the kids on the street, even if it was midnight"... major desires are "a whole bunch of money all at once" and "a man I could be proud of; a man who makes me feel good—like a baseball player"...*

The Infielder used to have some kind of parties at his hotel room after the games. You know, because of their curfew, players couldn't be out of their rooms after twelve—but as long as they were *in* the hotel room, it was cool. There would be three or four other players in the Infielder's room, and they would get to playing cards and drinking. Then somebody would call a girl, and she'd bring four more with her. If there were more girls than guys, somebody would holler down the hall and get a few more players. You know.

Pretty quick there'd be kissing and hugging, and I would just be sitting there looking. I could just sit there and look all night at some of those goings-on. (Laughs.) I mean, they'd be really getting down. Getting *down* right there.

Not the Infielder and me, though. I always have to have a little privacy. The Infielder would urge it on, but I still wouldn't do it. He didn't get mad. He'd just find us another room.

By that time of the morning, he was usually tipsy. And I was, too. So when we'd get a room alone, he had a thing about us taking a bath or shower. He would like to take bubble baths together in the tub and play with the bubbles. We never could make it in the shower because he was so tall. And getting down in the bathtub was too sloppy; it would mess up my hair. (Laughs.) The soap would get all over me. You know, we'd always be wrapped up in those big towels afterwards.

The Infielder was just too much. He was a lover from his heart. We went together about three years, and he was separated from his wife all that time. I would see him every time his team came to town, but he would visit me during the off-season every once in a while, too. First thing we'd do every time he came was go to bed. First thing. (Laughs.) You know, we were just comfortable with each other after going out together so long. As soon as he'd call me, I'd go over to his hotel and we'd right away get in our big bath towels. And of course he always brought his sex movies with him. Every time.

Those movies were just fine. Oh, a few bothered me a little because he would try to do with me what the people were doing in the movies: a bunch of different, crazy positions. (Laughs.) I'd let him try, sure. There was this one movie where a lady and man had a position that the Infielder and I could just *never* get right. They were kind of all twisted in their bed, and we could never get it right. Or the Infielder would tell me to stop. And he'd get up and turn the movie projector back to the beginning of the film. He'd run that film over and over, but we never did do it the way they were doing it.

He had that projector with him all the time, but always with new movies. Oh, he had a lot of different movies.

He even took pictures of me. Wonder if he still has my pictures? He'd snap me in the bathtub, or on the bed. Always nude. And a lot of times I didn't even know he was taking those pictures. Didn't bother me; it was okay. Then when he got them developed, he'd always show them to me. I don't mean movies, just regular snapshots.

When he showed the movies in his hotel room, he'd sometimes invite a few other players and their girlfriends to watch with us. He and I would always be sitting on the bed, and the rest of them would have pillows on the floor. Sometimes when the movies got going pretty good, the other couples would start getting down—right there on the floor. And I just stayed on the bed and watched them. I really did.

The Infielder would just sit alongside me grinning and looking and sometimes taking pictures. Nobody minded us watching them. Or him taking pictures. You know, those people on the floor were in a different world by that time; the last thing they thought about was him taking pictures.

The other people in the room were other players and their dates. Usually black dudes with white girls. Once there was this white dude up from a farm club, and he had a black girl with him. There were no problems there between the girls or anybody. Always had a fine time—talking, drinking, playing cards, although I don't play cards. And, of course, he would show his movies every night.

Usually, we'd go straight from the ball park to a bar and then to his room or some other player's room. And the couples would start coming in. There was one night when the Infielder had a bunch of really good movies.

One shows an orgy with four or five couples, all hooked up together. Then the next movie just had a man and his woman in different positions. One had a cat and a woman, then another a dog and a cat. He had so many of them, I forget what they were all about. But I do remember that most of them were pretty good.

I thought a lot of them were funny, but I remember once that the movies started getting to me. You know, I wondered when he and I could start to get it on. (Laughs.) You know, when were the other people going to leave his room and go home? I mean, I was ready. Gee, it was four o'clock in the morning already, and he had to play ball in the afternoon. And shit, *I* had to go to work, too. We hadn't seen each other for a while either, so naturally we were going to do something besides look at each other all night. (Laughs.)

The movies were still going on the wall and two other couples were still getting down together on the floor. But when they finally finished—the people, not the movies—they went out of the room and left the Infielder and me alone. Finally. I was glad, too, because it really was getting kind of embarrassing watching them—I mean the people—all that time.

He told me not to look. But it was hard not to. One couple had got up off the floor and was balling in a chair. I really didn't know what to look at first—the movies or the people. My eyes just kept going around and around the room. (Laughs.) It all seemed to be so funny that I nearly laughed out loud, but the Infielder kept telling me, "Ssshh. Now you be quiet."

Sex to me *is* sort of fun. I enjoy it. But depending on the person I'm with, it can be a serious, important thing to me. That's how it was with the Infielder. With him, the whole thing was beautiful. He treated me much differently than other men did. He'd always rub me down nice in the bath or shower, and we'd play and wrestle in our big towels, and we'd have pillow fights. One thing would lead to another, and it would be just beautiful. You know. And whenever we had a good, good night together, he would normally hit a home run the next day. But a lot of times he didn't hit one. (Laughs.)

167 *sue ann*

He was the first man who made sure that I was really taken care of in bed. He did everything to me that could be done. Everything. *Everything.* He did it all, and I did it all. Like I say, everything.

That man could really exhaust you, yes, he could. I'd be pooped. He could make it with me all night long if I would let him. But I wouldn't, because lots of times I had to go to work in the morning. And he had to do his work, too.

()

The Outfielder didn't like to go out. He just liked to go straight home from the ball park and turn the TV on and watch the news programs—especially if he'd hit a home run or done something special that night. He'd want to sit there and look at himself on TV while I fixed him something to eat. Oh, sometimes another player would come by, and the two of them would sit around and talk about a bunch of stupid stuff while I was just sitting around waiting. They would just talk stupid, childish stuff that was really boring to me. Or two or three other players dropped by to play cards. They played a lot of cards. But I'd always wait until they left.

We'd been going out about two weeks when I started sleeping with him, and that would be just about every night. He was a quiet, shy, romantic dude, and very gentle. The funny thing about him, though, was he liked to have all his sex on the couch. Always on the couch, and always with the TV on. (Laughs.) Especially sports programs. Really.

He'd have the news on, or the sports, or Johnny Carson. But I'm quite sure he wouldn't be looking at the set while we were getting down on the couch. I guess he just liked to have the noise in the background.

I always asked him to turn it off, but he wouldn't. He said he wanted the light from the TV. (Laughs.) I told him okay, but told him to turn off the TV and just switch on some regular light in the room. But he said a regular light would be too bright for him. (Laughs.) But I enjoyed it anyway. I never felt like I was competing with the TV for his attention. It was on, that's all. Just on.

The Infielder was more of a man than the Outfielder. In every way, even in conversation. I know that the Infielder had his movies and his parties, but he was always more concerned with me than the Outfielder was. The Outfielder was more interested in hitting the ball the next day. Oh, he wanted me to be satisfied, but normally he'd get his satisfaction first and then later wonder if I made it, too. If I didn't, he'd go back in.

Usually, if a man doesn't satisfy me, I just don't go out with him anymore.

()

I was talking to some sportswriter in the corridor near where the players got on the field, and one of the players on my Outfielder's team comes walking toward me flipping a ball in the air.

He said to me, "I heard there was a black girl working this area tonight." He talked to me for a couple more minutes, then said, "I would like to fuck you."

Just like that, and right in front of this newspaperman. It made me feel real bad. You know what I mean? And so we got into a real big argument—and this guy was one of the stars of that team. Why, today, he's one of the biggest men in the whole baseball world.

But a few minutes later, he came back to see me and apologized. He said that he and the Outfielder were good buddies, so he was sorry. He said he didn't know that I was tight with the Outfielder. Believe me, though, he never would have apologized if I *hadn't* been dating the Outfielder. He wouldn't have apologized at all. No sir.

If I'd said yes to him, I bet you he would have backed off and done nothing more than talk about me to the other

players. He did make me mad, and made me cry. I asked a
player to go and get the Outfielder out of the locker room so
he could help me stop crying.

O

Whenever the Infielder or Outfielder would take me to a
bar where the players went, I was usually the only black
woman in the place. A few times some of the white players
would come over to the table and say to me, "Who did you
come with? What are you going to do when you leave from
here?" I'd tell them, and they'd go away.

I remember sitting in these bars and looking around and
really getting bothered because I *was* the only black woman
there. Every time somebody new would come into the place,
I'd look at the door to see if it was another black woman
maybe. But usually it would be a black ballplayer with a
white girl. The longer I'd sit there, the more uncomfortable I
would feel. Very uncomfortable.

The Infielder always tried to make me feel mellow in
places like that, though. He would talk loud and get a group
together, and it would be all right for me then. I could relax
then.

The Outfielder was different. He didn't like to go out that
much; he hated having to get dressed up, and he didn't care
for crowds. Very seldom did we go out anywhere.

All the time in these places, I noticed that the other
women would be looking at me. They would stare. And I
don't like anybody to stare at me. *Nobody.* Not all those
white women, not anybody. Ooohh, it bugs me. I can *feel* a
stare.

I'd turn around and say, "What are you looking at?"

They'd say, "Oh, I wasn't really looking at you. Excuse
me."

You know, if something is wrong with the way I look, I like
people to tell me. Not just *stare.* I would go in the bathroom

to see if there was anything wrong with my face or my hair or whatever. I thought maybe I was talking too loud or not loud enough. Oftentimes I didn't feel very comfortable. I'd tell that to the Infielder, and he'd say, "Awww, don't worry about that. Have another drink. Enjoy yourself. Relax."

I used to see a few black players I knew there with white women, and I kind of wondered about that. I knew that some of these players were dating black women, because I'd seen them at parties. I couldn't understand why they didn't bring them, because that would have given me some one to talk to while the men were talking about left field and all this stuff, you know. But I never asked these players why they brought the white girls, and my Infielder wouldn't talk about it.

We would never stay in these places too long anyway, and that was just fine with me.

The few times I went with the Outfielder we'd usually just have one quick drink and hurry back to his place so he could watch the sports on TV. And with the Infielder, it was, like, maybe two or three drinks, a few fast dances and then over to his hotel room for the movies.

big sister

rosie... *thirty-five and one-half years old, five feet one inch tall, one hundred seven pounds. Find a sparrow, you find Rosie. Youngest of six kids of an Italian cabinetmaker who came from Calabria to Staten Island. Mother died before Rosie was four. At sixteen, Rosie quit high school because she was raped and pregnant. She and the infant boy lived with a brother. When the child was two, Rosie had him "adopted out." "I still feel the guilt. If I ever wanted to have a kid again, I'd adopt one. There's no way I'd bring a kid into this world. Life's too messed up." She has been a cocktail waitress last ten years. In love three times: At twenty-one first sweetheart was Korean veteran who "came back bitter and changed. I called it off." Next, an ex-Marine in Hawaii who "left me for a virgin. I even babysit for them now." Then, a couple of years ago, an older Navy officer. Visited his apartment one night, found another lady in his bed. "Now," she says, "I don't want any more involvements, and maybe that's why I dig athletes. They don't want any big hang-ups, either." She says she lives same way men do: "I should have been born a man; like, just because I'm with you tonight doesn't mean I want to be with you tomorrow night." She recalls going to bed with most of the roster of one National Football League team, some of its players "just as a courtesy." Can't total number of professional athletes serviced. "Give me a week to figure it out," she says, "I tried counting them all the other night and I fell asleep."*

Listen, I prefer athletes because I dig their bodies, what they're like—personalities—has nothing to do with it. I don't know if that's such a good idea. But I just go for the bodies. Not great big guys, although the first athlete I slept with was a great big center who I met at the bar I worked at. And not any of these rough little men who are trying to show some kind of false masculinity by being rough, like my father did when he'd slap me in the face. I call some of these types little wet rats. That's what I think of them. No. I just go for a good, firm athletic body. Mostly quarterbacks and receivers. It's not even an orgasm thing. Just digging the body. Firm, no flab.

And they know what they're doing in bed, most of them. They're groovy in bed. They've been around, you know. I very seldom don't get satisfied. I think it's knowing what you like, what pleases you. There was a time when I thought it was there and you did it and that was it. I didn't know what you got out of it. But I think that's something I've learned with these athletes. You know, it's getting rid of your inhibitions first.

It took me a while to do that, maybe because at first I had a complex about my body, that I was skinny. Especially when you get these guys with their gorgeous bodies, and you think, "Here's Little Miss Bones." Once I would get past that complex, I would be all right. And all of a sudden one day it dawned on me: They don't dig the body by itself; that's not why they're with me. They want to be satisfied in one way or another, and that's what it is. Know what I'm trying to say? And I just got over the complex. Of course, since I've gained weight I run around naked all the time. I love it.

As many players as I've been to bed with, I still, believe it or not, get embarrassed at times about telling them what I'd like them to do when we're together. If things aren't, you know, going the way I want them to or, you know, if I'm not getting close to where I want to be, then I'll probably say, "Do this, don't do that; I like this." You know.

But with athletes I don't usually have to say anything. I mean, I like just about everything. But there's still one thing that I don't go for, and I don't think I ever will. I don't know what they call it. It's what the Greeks do. I tried it once and it hurt so bad, you know, to start with. Then I got to thinking about it; it can't be too clean, you know.

Otherwise, though, I like to have a guy make love to me. I mean, I enjoy making love to him but I also want it back. Sometimes it's like, you know: "Here I am, come and get me." And he's laying there, and you've gotta get him all worked up and everything else; but he's not working you up. And that's not really fair. This is why if that sort of thing happens with a player, I avoid sex with him after that. It's like who needs it? I don't want to have to do all the work all the time; I don't want to be the aggressor all the time. I enjoy doing it, if I'm getting it back. Sometimes you just have to wonder: What am I here for? But I don't think I've really felt too often that these athletes are using me for sex. A couple times I can remember, yes.

There was this one player who in a sense put me down, and I had been super-good to him. I'd put him up in my place and everything else. We were almost like family, you know? We had just a very close relationship; it may even have been like he was a little brother to me, or whatever. But this one time he got super-drunk, and I don't think he would ever do this to me sober. I guess he was trying to impress a buddy. I wasn't home, and he just, boom, broke in. When I got back here to my apartment, I just flipped. I didn't talk to him for months afterwards.

But no matter what may happen with any of these guys we're always friends afterwards. No matter even if he's with me tonight and another girl tomorrow night. I wouldn't care. We'll still get along.

I don't like to hurt people's feelings. I mean, sometimes if a player I know asks me to go to bed with another player as a favor, well, I'll sometimes do it. But it's gotta be if I want to. Like, I can always say no. This one local player friend was with a guy from a visiting team and wanted to fix me up on a date type thing. I don't think he even asked me to go to bed with the visitor. So it was my choosing when I did go to bed with him.

Then there's like a courtesy thing. If there's a player I know and he really seems to need a little satisfying, okay. Just as a courtesy. Like, there's this one player I really wanted to be with when I first met him. I thought he was cute and everything else. And I thought, okay, groovy. So we got it on, but it wasn't that super-great. It was what I made it, not what he did. So after that we became just friends mostly. But there were a few times afterwards when he happened to be around and, okay, fine, we did it. There was no big thing. I really didn't want to be in bed with him. He wanted to be with me, but I didn't really care whether I was with him or not. Just courtesy. It's hard to say no when you've already been there sometimes.

I have a real good relationship with most of the guys. With some of the veterans I guess it's like a brother-sister thing. But the N.F.L. rookies coming in now are less caring. I don't know how to put this, but they just go wild. It's like a kid away from home for the first time. I don't really think half of them know how to treat people.

Still, there are a few good rookies, nice ones, coming into pro football, and lately I have been going out with some younger guys. The rookies I do go out with don't get out of line or bother me. I'm trying to think who I was with this year that was a rookie. Well, uh, maybe he was a rookie last year. I can't remember. (Laughs.)

()

There were two married guys on this old A.F.L. team that I'd been playing around with. The first one I met the first year the team came to town. But he was hurt the second year, so that's when I met the second guy. I can't remember if they were quarterbacks or receivers, but they weren't linebackers or guards or, you know, centers or anything like that because they had no flab. One was, uh, a . . . oh, I forget what the hell they were.

Anyway, the third year both of them show up, and the second player knew I'd been with the first one. The first one—let's call him Joe—didn't know about the second one—uh, Bill—though, and they were tight friends. Which I didn't realize.

It was Thanksgiving week. In fact, I fixed up half of the visiting team with dates that week. About twenty of them. What the hell, they're gonna be here for a couple of nights or whatever and they're all looking for action. At this bar I worked at, girls are just flocking in when they know there are football players around. And all you got to say, "He's a football player." And, zip, they're on. It was kind of nice to see everybody sitting with girls all night, you know. Everybody got more or less paired off.

As a cocktail waitress all I could do was introduce them. Whatever they do from there is their business. I don't care. I don't know what's gonna happen. It's none of my affair.

There have been a few times when I introduced a girl to a player and he said to me later, "Geez, why didn't you tell me about that broad?" You know: "What a filthy house," or "Jesus Christ, she won't leave me alone." But it's always been like that. Hey, when you put someone down everybody right away wants to pick them up. And I just figure, hey, find out for yourselves, fellas. Why should I say anything? Nobody listens, anyway.

But let me get back to these two particular visiting players. Joe calls me when the team comes in that Thanksgiving week. To me he was the superstud of the whole damned works. His call blew me away, you know, because I hadn't seen him for two years. And when he called me I knew right now who it was.

He had this tantalizing voice, and to me he was the perfect man. I mean, he was beautiful to look at and (laughs) he was hung like a *horse*. I mean, he knew what to do with it and everything else. I mean, I could sit and listen to him talk all day long. I loved his voice. In fact, I always said I wouldn't quit playing around until he quit playing football, because I wouldn't want to miss out on any of it. And when he called me, he made a date for the next night after I got off work. And I thought, oh my God, what am I going to do when the other one, Bill, shows up, because I really dug him, too. I mean, I loved these two guys. They were beautiful.

Bill comes into the place I worked first and has dinner there. I didn't know what to do. I fed him and everything, and when he finished his dinner I said, "Do you want anything else?"

He says, "No, just you for dessert."

And I'm thinking, "Oh, my God, what am I gonna do? How do I say anything to him?" I never really would play with two guys on the same team because I never thought it was too cool. I'd wait for one to leave the team, you know. I didn't know what to do, and Bill just hung around me all night long.

I kept trying to fix him up with different girls. And then Joe walks in. You could spot him just like this: Instant beauty. I went up to meet him and we came back to where Bill was. Joe says to me, "How does it feel to have two of the best guys on the same team?" And they're looking at each other.

I said, "You mean you knew it all the time?" And Joe says, "Sure. He asked me for your phone number, so I had to give it to him."

I felt really bad because I loved them both. They were two different types of people but both super-great. I mean, they're both still great friends of mine. I still get messages, you know. They're both out of football now, but I still get messages whenever they come to town.

So Joe, the guy I had the date with after work, floats around the place all night long. I figured, you know, he knows what time I get off and I don't care. Half the guys on the visiting team start coming up to me, because they all knew the story, and they'd say, "What's he doing with *that* girl?"

But I said, "Leave it alone. He'll be back to me at two o'clock. Everything'll be groovy." And I kept introducing Bill to every girl who walked in the place. I wanted to get *him* fixed up because I didn't want to leave him without a girl. And he kept saying, "No. I'm coming home with you, too." You know, he had plans to take me on after Joe finished.

I said, "No, I've never done that." I mean, you couldn't handle anyone else after Joe. Forget it. For three days I'd be laid up. Worn out.

But I couldn't put off Bill. I'd introduce him and he'd sit with a girl and have a drink with her and dance with her. Next thing I knew, he was right back in my corner. I'm thinking, "What am I gonna do?" So it comes two o'clock, and sure enough—the dummies—I got both of them drunk, you know, without thinking. And Bill walks out with the girl that was living right next door to me. I hated her guts. I was so mad.

Then Joe comes over. He said he knew what would happen, that he was going to wait for me all along. "Why should I go with anybody else?" he says to me. "You're the best in the place." Sure enough, there it was. I just figured that if I wasn't that good, he wouldn't have hung around all night. And the next night the other dummy—Bill—called me, you know, and I got together with him.

I've had some players introduce me to their friends as "the best around" and things like this. And I think I probably am. I think maybe one reason is I enjoy sex so much and I let it be known. I just don't have any inhibitions when I'm in bed. And I can get pretty noisy. A friend of mine who lives two doors down came up to me one morning and she says, "You better shut your windows at night when you're playing games."

I said, "Oh, my God." I just don't think about it.

()

I don't have a technique. I really don't know what I do in bed that's so important to these guys. Maybe it's because I can last with them all. Usually I can outlast them all night. I'll go as long as they want to—unless it's that one *thing* I said that I don't like.

Hell, I don't hesitate to go down on them. I enjoy it. In fact, I dig watching a man squirm. I really do. That turns me on I think, more than anything else. And if they want to go down on me, fine. If they don't, fine. Sometimes it bores me because some men don't really know what they're doing. I had a girlfriend who used to fall asleep when this one guy went down on her. That's all the guy wanted to do. And she fell asleep. It bored her, you know. You can only go for so much of that.

I like to make the rounds, you know, and try this and try that. I'm still waiting for somebody to teach me something I don't know. But I don't feel I really know all there is to know. I don't like to go to bed with a guy and just, you know, get it on and off. I like to lay around, talk to him, take a shower with him. Things like that.

It's usually too slippery in the shower, though. I've tried, you know; you really can't move around. You're slipping and sliding. Especially in a tub shower. Now maybe a stall shower would be better. First person I ever took a shower with was a football player—that superstud Joe. He used to ride me piggyback down the stairs to the shower. (Laughs.) It was fun.

There's only one other guy who came close to being as good as Joe. You know, the kind of a guy who prepared you, who worked with you to get some feeling into it. And sometimes it takes me a long time to get ready. Like last night I was going for three hours, and the guy came back this morning at ten o'clock. (Laughs.) And I said, "Oh, no." I mean, every time we turned around we started again. It was, you know, just one of those things. And he was only twenty-four years old. He's got a beautiful body, you know. He told me I've got a beautiful body. Not a football player, just a real sweet kid. And he's living with a girl. (Laughs.)

By now, I know what really turns me on. It depends, though, on the person. Like I love to have my shoulders kissed, right in around my neck and shoulders. And I just dig hands going over my body in a very soft way. Things like this, you know. I can't stand the rough stuff. It doesn't turn me on; it just turns me off. But if somebody's super-gentle with me, I love it. And that's what was so great about Joe.

He was super-tender, and he never changed from year to year. He worked you into it with all the foreplay. The whole bit. But he was rough when he had to be. I mean, sometimes I like to really get it on. There are times when I dig a deep thrust, or whatever you want to call it. But he wasn't rough with his hands or his mouth. He treated a body like it should be treated. And I found that most men like that *same* kind of treatment.

But there was this girl I knew once who I guess really dug the rough stuff. It didn't come from her own mouth, but I heard it from different players. I mean, not just football players, but from a few hockey players, too. They said she wanted to be beat up. Well, maybe not beat up, but slapped around a bit. She was evidently one of those people who get their kicks like that, I guess.

Most of the players I knew just didn't enjoy that. They weren't that type of person. I confronted her with it, you know, because I really liked the girl. She's a beautiful person. Heart of gold, everything. Good-looking girl, but you know, she came in one day with bruises all over. I said, "What the hell happened to you?" And she mentioned some guy's name. And I thought, no way; I know this guy too well. He's like a Teddy bear, you know. There was no way.

But she said he beat her up because she wouldn't go to bed with him. And I'm thinking that you don't go to a man's apartment to start with if you're not going to, you know, lay down with him. But I let her talk and I didn't contradict her in any way. I mean, this guy had so many things going for him, why would he have to beat up a girl?

I asked him about this one time. He said, "Hey, you know, she's kind of freaky. She wants to be slapped around. That's how she gets her kicks." But she wouldn't admit it to me. Then I heard the same thing from a hockey player, and I thought, hey, they can't *all* be wrong. And then one guy on a visiting team heard about her and got together to see if it was true. And it was true.

I told her she needed help. "That's not normal," I told her. I liked her enough to want her out of that type of thing. But she swore it wasn't true. She finally got married. Very happily.

()

I don't think I've ever been really sorry about sleeping with so many different athletes. I mean I don't think I'm a nymphomaniac. I really don't. I can understand, I guess, a man getting horny without being near a woman. I don't know, it's just part of their nature, but I don't get that way.

People say, "Geez, I'm horny," but I couldn't get horny without thinking of a particular person. Just thinking about sex wouldn't, you know, super-turn me on. It has to be an individual guy for me. Like if I was with somebody who was super-good, I'd think, "Geez, I'm in the mood to be with him tonight." But just to want to go to bed all the time, well, no. In fact, I've read in different books that there's no such thing as nymphomania. But I guess that if I saw a different guy every night who turned me on, and it was convenient, I wouldn't hesitate to go to bed with him.

I like the guy that's tall and lean. And he's gotta be clean—definitely clean. You know, the athlete type. Of course, if you saw what I was going out with tonight—a plumber—you might wonder what I mean by this clean stuff, but my plumber doesn't have time to go home and change after work. And I wouldn't go to bed with him until he got in the shower.

It's not all sex, really. Sometimes I just like to cuddle up in bed, you know. Not to sleep alone; I'm scared of the dark. (Laughs.) I really am. I just love to curl up around somebody. And when a big man is holding me, I feel protected. I feel like, you know, it's not just the sex but maybe he cares a little bit—even if I'm not in love with the cat. It's just kind of nice to know that somebody gives a damn once in a while.

But with short men it's just different. I go out with them but I don't go to bed with them. I kind of think my father— that little guy—was a superstud, too, the way my mother was shelling out with us six kids, you know. And probably if she hadn't died young there'd have been six more.

But I don't know what my thing is with little guys. Years ago, before I started with athletes, I went out with this short guy and I really liked him. He was a fantastic dancer and a lot of fun. When it came time to go to bed with him, though, I couldn't get it on. In fact, I got out of bed. I don't know what it was. I had a super-crush on him before, and I just don't know how to explain what it was about being with him in bed. But I looked and there he was, a dinky little guy, and he kind of reminded me of a wet rat. And I've never been with one since. Maybe I don't feel protected with them. I don't know, I mean, I've even been with a guy almost seven feet tall, if you can feature that.

He was a pro basketball player. White guy, of course. Always. This was a couple of years ago. He was sitting in the bar. He wasn't the best-looking man in the world—not even at the bar that night—but I remember watching him because he looked so bored. And I think I kept looking at him because I got curious to see if (laughs) he was big all over. You know, he was so tall.

A couple of girls had gone over to sit with him, one on each side, but he still sat there completely bored. And I went over to him and said, "Hey, you know you really look bored."

And he said, "I am."

So I picked up his drink and moved him down to the bar next to where I was working and, you know, we started talking. Everybody was teasing me about it. How big he was and all. And I kept thinking, I wonder if he really is big all over? (Laughs.)

There was only one way for me to find out. He asked me if he could, you know, come home with me. I told him I didn't know how to drive and that he'd have to get his own way back to his hotel. I told him that a taxi would cost him a lot. He didn't care. And I thought, "Hey, if you want to spend the money, that's fine with me." I figured he must want to be with me bad enough if he's gonna spend the money.

So we came home, and he *was* just as big. (Laughs.) I remember thinking—oh, this is terrible—when I first touched it. "Oh, hello. Where's the vaseline?" And it had been a little while since I'd slept with anybody. At first I felt maybe I didn't want to bother. Then I thought, "No, it's been so long, let it hurt." (Laughs.)

He was really a nice guy. Very soft, very gentle. I think that gentle touch was what had turned me on first anyway. While he was sitting on the bar stool he kissed me, and I thought, "Wow," 'cause I could barely feel his lips and it was beautiful. So I figured I better try it out. It *did* hurt. I don't know if it was longer or wider; it was just every which way big, you know. It hurt, but I wasn't sorry.

There was, I guess, one time when I regretted going to bed with an athlete, wishing I didn't. It was the week of an all-star game. I'd been playing around with this one guy who was a beautiful person. Super-big, nice guy. I think I liked his personality more than anything else. I enjoyed being with him. But another guy on this football all-star team who wasn't half his size comes up with this jazz "I'm going to steal you from him." And he said it right in front of the guy.

I thought that, well, if he had the guts to come up with it that way, maybe, you know, I'd give it a whirl. So this second guy—he's a quarterback—phones and tells me to come to his room. I thought, "Oh, well. What not?"

I started changing my mind, but some friends, some other players, drag me out of my apartment, drive me to the quarterback's, carry me out of the car and into his room and then threw me right in the middle of his bed. Just barged right in.

I was super-smashed, really drunk. And I thought, "Oh, well, what the hell. I'm here. I might as well." You don't go into a guy's room and not play around. And to me it was the biggest waste of time in my life. It was like, boom boom. I didn't even know he was alive. I couldn't feel anything. And to me he's always been the poorest excuse for a man I've ever known. And I just, you know, wish it had never happened.

I remember afterwards, he didn't even want me to stay there. He had this attitude that he was God, you know. He was Mister Great. At the time, in the early sixties, he was pretty big. And it was like, "You can't stay here lady. I'll get in trouble tomorrow morning."

I'm so damned drunk I have no way of getting back home, so I say, "Call me a cab." He did and wanted to give me money for the taxi and I told him to shove it. I told him I didn't need his money. I'd pay for my own damned cab and I didn't need anything from him. Nothing, you know?

Sometimes when I drink I get more lovable or something. I don't even think about it, you know. I just want to do it. The hell with it. I know I'm completely uninhibited when I'm drunk. Hey, everything's groovy. The lights stay on, the mirrors are hung. I just don't even care.

Like I was sitting in a bar downtown a couple weeks ago and having a great time. I was with a girlfriend and half-smashed. Everybody was coming up to me because I'm a very happy drunk. And all of a sudden these two baseball players walked in. I don't know what happened, but I zonked out on this one guy and that was it.

Now this is sweet: I think I like Libras. I've met three of them in the last three weeks that were all good. (Laughs.) This baseball guy was really nice, you know, and he wanted me to go back to his room with him. And I'm wondering how I'm going to get home the next day, so he finally says, "Well, let's go to your place."

Like, I've been talking to him for a half hour and I know he had to think I was crazy, besides being drunk, and I tell him, "Okay, my place. But on one condition: That you don't leave right after you fuck me. You've got to spend the night." (Laughs.)

And he says, "I don't have to be anywhere until noon tomorrow."

I said, "Good." He was really, really sweet. And he wanted to take my phone number with him. He said he could keep my number because he wasn't married. But even if he had been, I would have given it to him.

I mean, even if the athlete is married and he appeals to me, it's a matter of if I want him, I want him. In a way, I'm more comfortable not having to worry about long entanglements. Once in a while, if I really dig the guy, I'd like to have maybe a little entanglement. You know, have the same guy around. But I never know if I want that with a guy until after I've been to bed with him.

Still, I get bored quickly with a guy unless he's got a super personality and can keep me, you know, interested in a lot of things. I think that's why I don't get married; I just haven't found the man that can keep my interest long enough. And emotionally—well, I've been there a few times and I've been hurt and I'm not gonna be hurt again. So now I just shut off my emotions. That's why I think I don't see any particular guy for too long a time, you know. I may enjoy going to bed with one guy, but I just don't keep him around long enough to care. I mean, hey, you know, I sleep with all different kinds of people, but I always try to make sure I know a little bit about them. And at least I make sure they're clean and I'm not gonna catch anything. Knock on wood, I never have.

185   *rosie*

O

I've let a few football players who are friends use my apartment if they need to sometimes. You know, there are times a guy has nowhere to go, and he wants to take a girl somewhere and be alone. Whatever he wants to do, you know, if I really like and trust the guy, why I'll let him come over. Especially if he's from an out-of-town club. I mean, why pay a motel bill?

I've put up a couple rookies that way for a couple weeks. I enjoy cooking for them, things like this. I eat better that way, too, because I never cook for myself. And I don't take any money from any of these guys. They're friends. And I don't sleep with them when they're over either. You know, no sex. I had a couple of rookies staying at my place one time. Both single guys. One slept in my spare room and the other with me in my bed. But I didn't even ball him the whole time he was there. It was just one of those things.

Before I let a player bring a girl over, I've got to make sure I know he won't let the girl rip me off one way or another. It's not important that I know the girl. I don't care who they are; that's the player's business.

I've seen some types of girls in sports bars I don't care for particularly. There's one in particular; in fact, I think she's the only person I've ever completely disliked. She's maybe just twenty-one now. She's the type that hangs on, won't leave a guy alone, constantly calling, constantly bothering a person, making up stories, putting people down—but in a way very cunning and conniving. I mean, really cunning. She could be supersweet when she'd first meet you, and you think, "Oh, she's a nice kid." Until you get to know her.

She's a back-stabbing bitch, and that's the way I look at her. And half the guys I know can't stand her. But yet, and this bothers me a lot, these guys put her down, but when there's nothing around they go after her. And they wonder why they're being bugged. You know, this is what I don't understand. I've warned some players about her, but, hey, you know, I always said, "A stiff dick has no conscience."

But I do insist that a player takes care of my place when he has a girl over with him. Lots of times I'm not even home when a couple comes over. But if I am, it doesn't matter, doesn't bother me, doesn't bother them. I've never felt jealousy when a guy's with another girl when I'm around. I figure there's another player around the corner anyway. I just always prided myself that I always got to them first. (Laughs.)

rachel... *twenty-six years old; five feet four inches
tall, one hundred eighteen pounds, blue-gray eyes that
seem mostly to glance down at a long chin; blonde,
Southern California high school homecoming queen who
always wanted mother "to tell me I was pretty. But all
she'd say was that I was a nice girl." When boys told her
she was pretty, "I wouldn't believe them. They wanted
something." Used to tell mother, "Go up and hug daddy
and give him a kiss. Say you love him. Normally she
wouldn't do that." Former husband, a muscular regular
with major league baseball team, was sports hero at
Rachel's high school. Began dating him at sixteen, slept
with him (Marvin) within six months. "I said, 'I'm not a
virgin anymore.' And he said, 'yah.' And I wasn't really
happy about it." Married him at twenty with feeling of
nervous naivete. Physically contradictory: Angelic, yet
starlet-sexy. Went from Plain Jane wardrobe, "all blues,
all reds, all solids," to way-out, many-hued wildness.
Marriage brought two daughters, lasted four years, sort
of. After divorce, she began playing the football game.
Word among ex-husband's teammates was that Rachel
was sleeping with everybody. "I came across as
something I wasn't," she says. "But that doesn't bother
me anymore. I knew I was in limbo looking for my own
personality." The pain, if one can get past the sensuality,
is evident.*

It was before we were married. I was still in high school and
we were going steady. He had signed a major league contract
and was with his club in L.A., so I went up to see him. We'd

always been truthful with each other, and I asked him if he'd been dating. So he went through a list of girls, you know, just naming this one and that. He couldn't remember one of their last names. Then he said he'd gone to bed with one named Peggy, and that he and a married player had taken two girls back to their rooms. I got mad at first. Then I thought, well, we're not married yet and I don't have a ring on my finger; all I have is the verbal word that we're going to get married. So I said to him, okay, we'll just forget it.

And when the club was ready to leave after a series in the area, I went up to his hotel room to help him pack. I noticed on the right side of his suitcase there were a bunch of letters—and not all of them from me because I can tell my handwriting. And Marvin was never too cool about hiding things. He casually picked them all up and moved them to the left side of the suitcase. Very casually; I'm not supposed to notice. I just went and grabbed three of the letters, and he went for me and tried to get them. I held them behind my back and we argued and then I just went across the room and read them.

One was from a girl named Sally that said, "The showers are sure lonely without you. Hurry back." Another letter was from a coach's daughter he'd told me that he broke up with. She told him that she was sorry she couldn't make it down to spring training, but maybe next time. And then this other letter from the girl with the last name he forgot. She goes in her letter, like, "The lights are down low and the music is playing and the bed's ready. The only thing that's missing is Big M, and that's you."

()

When I was pregnant with our second child, I missed most of spring training, and about a year later I heard a rumor about what Marvin had done there with one of the booster club members. Woman I knew, too, because Marvin and I had doubled with her and her husband all the time. And I knew Marvin liked her. He once told me, "She is the most beautiful woman I have ever seen." She came down to the training camp without her husband. And Marvin and one of the pitchers and this woman and another girl go to a sauna bath together. And they played kissy face. That's what I call it. They did it, right there in the sauna. Somebody, I forget who, told me. But I didn't mention it to Marvin.

I eventually confronted the pitcher, told him I knew all about what the four of them had done. And he said, "How did you know about that?" I said, "I'll never tell." He really just blew it by confirming it to me.

This call comes at home one day while Marvin's on the road. The woman on the phone says, "Is this his sister?" And calm and cool I said yes, it was. So she left her first name and phone number and asked me to have him call her when I heard from him. I hung up and called him long distance. I gave him the message that such and such a girl called from Boston, that she said he'd know her even without a last name.

Marvin said, "Rachel, are you serious? I don't know anybody like that. Are you trying to drive me crazy?"

I said, "*Me* trying to drive *you* crazy? I think you're driving *me* crazy."

He said, "I don't know what you're talking about."

But I went ahead and gave him her number. A few minutes later he calls me back and says that these two guys were at a baseball party in Boston and thought it would be a good joke for this girl to call players all over the country. That they thought it was a really good joke. I don't think I believed what he said. But I guess I accepted it.

()

It wasn't until we went to analysis that I was really able to figure out why he'd been acting that way so long. What it was was he didn't want to be married. Subconsciously. And that's why he was being mean to me all the time. He knew he was acting mean, but he didn't know why. And he wouldn't admit to himself that it was simply because he didn't want to be married. He was just mean to me on purpose. What he wanted me to do was to leave him—which I finally did. He wanted the breakup to be my fault, not his.

For a long time, most of the time he was in the Majors, I suspected he was going out on me. When he was on the road I would call his room at two in the morning and he wouldn't be in. And he was supposed to be in the room. Not at a bar. And later he would tell me he was in another player's room in a poker game, or else he would give me the excuse—like when he was in Minneapolis—that he was staying at the house of some guy from the Twins he knew. Or that he and a group of players were just out visiting. And these were just phoney excuses, you know. You can't say: Oh, yeah, you're a liar; you were out with someone else.

Then when he'd come home he'd deliberately pick a fight. And he wouldn't have anything to do with me. There was one period of about four months that there was nothing physical between us at all. Like when the club was home once he took off after a game with one of our pitchers, also a married guy, and did not come in until four in the morning. I asked him where he had been, and he told me it was none of my damned business.

There were always big arguments. He was always mad at me if I got to the airport late to pick him up when the team came home. One day I was in such a hurry to get him on time that I had on two different shoes. I was trying to decide which shoes to wear. I tried half a dozen shoes on and I got to the airport and I was walking to the gate where the ball club was and that's when I realized I had two different shoes on. I looked down and, oh, I just about died. I wondered how many people had seen that I had two different shoes on. So I just took them off and walked barefoot the rest of the way to the gate. But I was five minutes late and I couldn't see him at the gate. So I thought he was on the team bus going back to the hotel where they usually dropped off some guys. I got back in my car and drove all the way to the hotel. The bus was there but he wasn't, and some of the players told me he was still waiting at the airport. And I thought, oh, no.

I called the airport and had him paged and told him what had happened. Naturally he was mad, so I went and picked him up. And the whole way home he didn't speak to me. When we got home the kids had left a tricycle out on the sidewalk, so he picked it up and swung it across the garage into the wall. Then I was walking into the house and dropped my purse and everything fell out and I was trying to pick it up, and he was hovering over me. After I picked up the stuff I started going up the stairs and dropped everything out of the purse again. That's how nervous he was making me.

He kicked his suitcases clear across a room and took off different articles of clothing, like his coat, and flung them. His coat and cufflinks and shirt and shoes and socks. Then he just lay down on the bed and looked at the ceiling. And I said, "What's the matter?"

And he said, "Nothing's the matter. Nothing." There was just no communication.

There were times in those bad four months that I would ask him why he wasn't making love to me. And I think he said that he just didn't like me anymore, that I would have to prove to him that I loved him before he would have anything to do with me anymore. He said I had to keep the house clean. He would get mad at me if I made too fancy a meal. Any nice thing I'd serve he would get mad at me, you know.

He'd say, "Why don't you just make a plain old hamburger sometime?" And I always made him good food. And I wasn't a sloppy housekeeper. Not that I was immaculate, but all of his complaining has made me still to this day nervous if the house isn't clean.

All these arguments and his staying out that one night and telling me it was none of my business where he was and these four months of nothing.... Well, one night I went out at four in the morning right after he pulled that stunt and I (laughs) just drove down to an all-night grocery store near our house and stayed in the parking lot. I just sat in the car and smoked and did nothing for a couple of hours, then I went back home.

He said, "Where have you been?"

I said, "None of your damned business."

He took off on a two-week road trip and I went out of town to visit a ballplayer's ex-wife. I was discussing with her everything that was going on. I told her I knew that Marvin was, you know, messing around on me.

She said, "Well, it's really about time you figured it out because he's been going out on you ever since I've known him, since you were pregnant with your first child. Remember when our husbands played together and were out of town and you told me to say hi to him for you?"

I told her that yeah, sure, I remembered. And then she said that they couldn't find Marvin to pass along my regards because, she said, Marvin was out fucking around.

"But I didn't have the heart to tell you then," she said. She told me he never wore his ring on the road. And I guess that's how he lost it—taking it off on the road all the time. He told me he flushed it down a toilet accidentally, that he'd left it on the sink in a bathroom and it went into the toilet. He never did get another ring. What's the difference? He would have taken a new ring off anyway the minute he got out of town.

She asked me where his club was playing. I told her they would be in Anaheim and Oakland and Minneapolis this trip—in Minneapolis two days and two or three nights. And she said, "If it's going to happen, it's going to happen in Minneapolis."

I said, "Really?"

And she said, "Yah." So she told me about this private detective and I went to him and he set it all up. They followed Marvin and they caught him.

It was scary for me going to see the private detective. He was kind of scary looking, too. When I talked to him at the first he said, "Are you sure you want to do this?" I told him yes, that I did, and I gave him a description of Marvin, his uniform number, who he roomed with, a copy of the itinerary, flight schedules, all that. I had to pay the man three hundred fifty dollars down, and he said he'd reimburse me whatever they didn't use. I really hadn't thought about how I'd explain spending that money to Marvin because I was sure that we were going to find him out, you know. I was just mad.

Still, even though I knew what was going on, I thought that well, maybe he's not playing around. Because when the private detective told me what they did find, it hit me like a brick. I was shocked. I really was.

It was only about two days until I heard from the private detective. I had to wait until Marvin got to Minneapolis. They caught him the first night there. And the detective called me and he says, "Well, we caught him." He said that he didn't have all the information yet but that he would soon get it. He wanted to know if I wanted him to do any more following, and I told him to try in a couple of more cities. They lost him once in Los Angeles and they never found anything in any other cities. But I did get a full report on what happened in Minneapolis. Right down to every detail I'll never forget it.

They had everything. They gave me the year and the make of the girl's car and the license number and where she had lived three years ago and her parents' telephone number and their address and her telephone number and address. Where she worked—she was a dental hygienist—and how much she made, where she banked, who her roommate was. And the color of her hair, and that she was a chronic gum chewer.

I even asked Marvin about that later and he said, "Chronic gum chewer? She doesn't even chew gum. I just asked her if she wanted some gum, and she took a piece for the first time."

I said, "Hey, c'mon." I mean, I had a complete mental picture of this gam. I even called her up and talked to her.

I waited until he was on a plane so there was no way she could get in contact with him—you know, so he wouldn't know he was being followed. He was on a plane heading for home when I called her. I just asked her if she knew Marvin was married, and she said that she did. I said, "Do you know he has a four-month-old child?" She said she didn't.

I said, "Did you know that when my child was two days old he left on a road trip and didn't call me for a week? When I called him in Minneapolis he told me to call back in an hour because he must have been with you?" She said she didn't know about that.

I said, "What does he say to you? That I'm a bitch or something?"

And she said, "No. Just that you two don't get along."

I said, "That's all he said? Nothing else?" She said that was all.

I asked her if she had any relations with him. She said, "What do you mean?"

And I said, "You know what I mean." She finally said yes.

I asked her why she went out with him. She said that he was nice and they were just friends and it was on a platonic basis. I said, "How can you say it's platonic when you've had relations with him. It's not platonic if you go to bed with him."

She said, "Yah. I guess you're right. I hope you don't think I'm some kind of whore or something."

I said, "No, I don't." I was really nice about it.

At first my impression was to hate her. You know, I was going to call her parents and tell them to get on their daughter's case and steer her right, that she was going around breaking up people's marriages. Then I thought that, no, I can't do that. Two wrongs don't make a right. So I just called her up and not her parents. And after that I think I phoned her once more.

I know Marvin continued to see her after that for a while. But she got married finally to her boyfriend. His name was Georgie. (Giggles.) Gee, I guess I knew just about everything about her. I mean, the reason I knew her boyfriend's name is that once she typed Marvin a note saying that Georgie was all upset about her seeing him but that Georgie would get over it and that she couldn't wait until Marvin made another trip in. Well, I'm a very suspicious person, and I would go through his pockets and his wallet. Just nosing around to see if I could find anything. And I found the note from her.

I went to see a lawyer after I got the private detective's report. We got all the paperwork done so that we could serve Marvin with divorce papers when he came in at the airport—back from that road trip. I went to the airport with this man, I guess you call him a process server. I told him that I was going to give Marvin the chance to tell me the truth. If he told me the truth, I wasn't going to serve him with the papers. But if he lied, I was. So I worked out signs with the man. Two fingers meant serve the papers. One, don't.

I had lost about seventeen pounds in those last couple of weeks. Weighed about one hundred ten. And I dressed differently. A lot of wives on our club were sort of young and kind of backwards as far as the styles went—you know, long dresses and skirts while minis were coming in. So I wore a mini to the airport. I went out and bought a velour mini-skirt. Cranberry velour (giggles).

I had to try it out first to see if I had the nerve to walk out in public. I never had worn a mini before so I had a cousin take me to a movie. I got out of the car and walked up to the box office and bought a ticket and walked in the movie. That was a big thing for me. I kept tugging the skirt down and asking my cousin if it didn't seem a little too short. He said that I looked great. But I still felt that I left part of my clothes at home.

At least I got practice walking in that skirt so I wouldn't feel too weird when I went to the airport. I guess I looked like a new woman that day. Like, one of the players coming off the plane saw me and asked his wife who I was. It was a whole new me.

I met Marvin and gave him a kiss and everything. Then right away I asked him where he had been on such and such a night in Minneapolis. He said, "In my room."

I said, "Well, I called you and you weren't in."

He said, "You didn't call."

I said, "Yes I did."

And he said, "I never received the call. And I was there."

I said, "No, you weren't there."

He said, "Oh, we aren't going through this shit again, are we?"

And I said, "Are you going to tell me where you were?"

He said, "I was in my room the whole time."

And I said, "Marvin, I'm going to ask you one more time. Tell me where you were." He just said, "Shit."

So I said, "Okay. Here's where you were." And I had, you know, memorized the whole report from the private detective. I started right from the beginning to the very end—telling him he left the game at such and such a time, walked out with one of the guys, left alone and went to her car. I gave him the color, make, license number. Told him they went to such and such a restaurant, had two drinks. Told him her physical description, that she was a chronic gum chewer and had bleached hair.

He said, "It wasn't bleached, it was frosted. And she's not a chronic gum chewer."

Actually, it was kind of funny, you know. Even the worst kind of situation can be that way sometime. So I kept giving him all this report as we walked in the airport. And suddenly he just stopped walking. I knew he was in shock. He never thought I was ever capable of doing something like that, hiring somebody. Which, I guess, was true. If my girlfriend hadn't suggested it, I probably wouldn't have done it.

He lit up a cigarette and said, "Now are you happy? Are you proud of yourself?"

And I said, "No, not proud of myself. But I know I'm not crazy like you say I am. Everything I've asked you about is

197   *rachel*

true, and you are a liar." I had a speech that was all planned out—telling him what I thought of him and how disappointed I was and how he disgraced our family and degraded us and made us seem like we were nothing, me and the two girls, and that I was sure he didn't care anything about us and how could he possibly say he loved us when he did things like that. I ended up by saying that he was nothing more than a male whore. And I held up two fingers to signal the process server. The man came over, and little did I know that he was a weasel.

He went over to Marvin and said, "I guess you know what this is?" And he sort of flung the papers, and Marvin almost slugged him. If he had, he would have had a lawsuit on his hands plus the divorce. But he didn't.

I just turned around and went over to the hotel where the visiting team had just come in and was staying. The Yankees. I had gone to school with one of the guys who was playing for them then, and I called his room and began crying and told him the whole story. He told me to calm down, that he would come to the lobby. We were on the phone for a long time, though, and while we were talking one of the pitchers on Marvin's club walks into the lobby to pick up Marvin's suitcases, which had come there from the airport. I guess Marvin was going to spend the night at this pitcher's house or something.

The pitcher sees me on the phone and walks over and—this shows you how they stick together—says to me, "Marvin didn't do what you say. He's not capable of doing that. He loves you, and I don't care what the detective says. The detective is lying."

Meantime, this guy from the Yankees is still on the other end of the line hearing all this. The pitcher keeps telling me that the detective's report is a whole farce, and I'm telling him that we have proof and everything. But the pitcher still denied Marvin did anything. It's incredible how they stick together like that. You know, they all do it and if one tells on another he knows he'll get told on, too. So they keep their mouths shut and stay safe. It's sort of like a pact they have.

I mean, I know why they all do it. They're gone two weeks a month and they say they get lonely. They need companionship, they say. After a game, they just don't feel like going back to their room and going to sleep. Alone. So they go somewhere and have a few drinks, and the girls are there. So why not? But I can't sympathize with that. I was home two weeks alone every month and *I* didn't screw around. I could wait. Why couldn't *he* wait? Until I got that detective's report I had been faithful. I wasn't looking for anything else.

While I'm standing there talking to the pitcher and still holding the phone with the guy from the Yankees on the other end, Marvin comes in. The pitcher sees him and says, "I'm telling you, I know Marv, and Marv still loves you."

And Marvin walks up to me and says, "Would you please talk to me?" I tell him there's nothing to talk about.

Over the phone the Yankee player is saying. "Talk to him. I'll be down in a minute." He hangs up and I put down the phone and walk into the bar with Marvin.

The guy from the Yankees comes in with his wife, so the four of us are sitting having a drink and talking about old times. But Marvin and I never really talked about anything. That was our problem: We never talked about anything. While we were sitting there, the cocktail waitress slipped some kind of card underneath my napkin. I didn't notice it for a long time until I started playing with my napkin. All of a sudden I found this card and turned it around and it said something like "Hi there, sweetie pie" or some cliche. There was a man's name and room number. And he asked me to call the room.

Marvin sees me looking at the card and reads it, too. "Who do you think sent this card?" he says. I told him I didn't know but maybe it was a guy sitting over in a corner giving me the eye.

So Marvin gets up and goes over to the guy and says, "Did you send this card?" The guy admits it and Marvin tears up the card in all sorts of little pieces and throws them in the guy's face and says, "This is my wife." The guy apologizes for making a mistake and the two of them start talking over there in the corner.

Marvin comes back and says, "You'll never guess who that guy is? He went to my elementary school."

Marvin wanted to take me back home, but I didn't want to go, so we just got a room there at the hotel. And he grabbed me and kissed me and told me how much he loved me. He said, "Please don't leave me," and "I can't live without you," and that sort of thing.

We spent the night at the hotel. The next morning when we were walking down the hallway, a ballplayer from the Yankees spots us and looks at Marvin and says, "You got yourself a good-looking one"—not knowing I was his wife. I just laughed.

I let him come back home that day. I still loved him and didn't want to really leave him. I asked him why he did it, and he told me he felt sorry for her. And I said, "Why don't you try feeling sorry for me? Why do you feel sorry for other people? How about me?"

He said, "Well, all she has in her life is skiing." And I got mad and kicked him out of the house and called my lawyer.

I told him, "I think I blew it. I went to bed with my husband last night and kicked him out of the house today."

He said, "That's all right because you can always say you did it in a moment of mental weakness."

We were separated off and on for the next eight months. Poor lawyer: I'd tell him I wasn't going through with the divorce, and he'd say: "You'll be back." And I was.

()

One day while we were separated there's this phone call from a woman with a foreign accent. She asked if Marvin lived at this number. I said, "Yes." And she hangs up. Fifteen minutes later she calls again and asks if Marvin the baseball player lives here. Again I tell her that he does and she apologizes for hanging up and says she didn't know he was married. I told her he was, for about four years, but now we were separated. She said she was sorry, but she didn't know about that. I told her a lot of people didn't.

I said, "By any chance are you a brunette?"

"Yes, I am," she said. "How did you know that?"

I told her that the girls he goes out with are usually dark-haired—except me and the blonde I caught him with in Minneapolis. And she was frosted anyway. And over the phone this woman tells me detail for detail what had happened between her and Marvin. I couldn't believe that she was doing it, and I let her go ahead. Actually, it was like punishing myself. She told me she'd been married in Europe in one of those old country arrangements, that she'd left her husband to live in New York and then she'd moved out here. She said Marvin was only the second man in her life. She said she'd been writing him at the ballpark for a year.

She said she was walking down the street in New York one day and saw this group of guys and asked them for directions. They were all ballplayers. She said Marvin started talking to her and invited her to come to the game that night and have dinner. She said she did. Apparently she was living in the same hotel where the team stayed. She told me that after dinner Marvin walked her to her room, and she thought that was going to be it. She said he sort of just shoved his way into the room, that he was really sort of aggressive toward her and she found him physically attractive.

So anyway they went on from there and made love or sex or whatever. She told me she got upset and cried to him that she might get pregnant. She said he told her she knew what she was doing, so shut up. And you know, I can't believe that he would talk that way to someone; I can't remember seeing that rudeness-toward-women side of him.

She said, "I don't know why I'm telling you this."

And I said, "I don't even know why I am listening."

We both were very honest with each other. I told her next time I saw Marvin I'd tell him she called, and I did. He admitted to the affair he had in New York with her. I gave him her phone number. And he said, "I don't want the number," and threw it away.

I was going to meet her, though. She was going to drive in and we were going to talk. She had told me she didn't have any girlfriends and that she was working for a married doctor who was making advances toward her. She said she didn't know what to do because she needed the job. She was asking *me* for advice. It was really weird. But I talked to her. I told her that, you know, she should tell the doctor that she was not interested in an affair with him. I said, "If you want to meet some people I'll introduce you."

I really felt sorry for her. Then my girlfriend said, "You have to be insane to meet this woman and help her. If you were anybody else, you'd want to kill her." I said that was probably true. So I never did meet her.

()

During these off and on months, I went to spring training camp with him. But we just didn't get along. I mean, I went back to him saying that if he wanted to screw around on me, it was all right. Just so he'd come home and be nice to me. And he told me it was okay if I put myself in these same circumstances, that I could go out to bars and stuff while he was on the road. I *was* going out. I had opportunities. But I still wanted to make Marvin happy.

I'd ask him what I could do to change. And he'd say, "I don't know, Rachel, I don't know." I was willing to do anything. But there was nothing I could do.

A pitcher's wife on our club told me that she absolutely would never go back with her husband if she caught him going out on her. I got opinions from a lot of the wives.

One said, "I can't tell you what to do. If you think you can handle a marriage under these circumstances, then stick with it." But nobody really told you to stay. You never got that.

I'm still friends with some of the wives now but I don't have anything much to do with them. One I just talk to on the phone or at a game if I see her. And there's an old friend from our days together in the minor leagues. She absolutely hated Marvin, thought he was the biggest shit in the world during the time our trouble was going on. With her now it's just hello, how are you, how are the kids, gee they're growing. That's about it. She became worried Marvin would be a bad influence on her husband.

A lot of the wives called me up and asked me if their husbands' names were on the private detective's report, and I said, "I'm not going to tell you anything. If you want to find out, hire your own private detective."

At first, you know, I thought of blowing the whistle on everybody. It was sickening. Like animals. They didn't have any respect for themselves or anyone else. But that was immediate bitterness. You know, like if they were lawyers instead of ballplayers, I would have hated all lawyers.

O

Just before our divorce, and for a while right afterwards, I got involved with this married football player, a guy from an American Football Conference team. It was hard for me to date at first because of my hate for men. If I felt I *needed* someone, I would give my ex a call. And he would be agreeable.

I would call Marvin up and discuss how weird I was because I couldn't do anything with anyone else. I couldn't do it because I was still old-fashioned in my thinking. Except with this football player, because how I felt towards him and how happy I was. But I didn't have any sex with him until *after* I found out he was married.

I met him in a bar. He was very good looking and very serious. I don't know what position he played; all I remember is that he was one of those guys who ran after the guy who had the ball. He didn't know Marvin but he'd heard of him.

He had told me his whole life story one night over dinner without mentioning he was married and had two kids—one of them just four years old. It was like, you know, when I caught Marvin going out on me. Really a mind blower. And when I found out about his marriage I started crying and everything. The football player said, "Let's go and have some coffee and discuss what never was said."

He sat down and told me about his two kids and took me home. I told him that I wasn't going to see him anymore. I was completely crushed, because I'd really been happy with this guy. Comfortable. He was what I always wanted and dreamed about. I had even called my mother and told her I met this fantastic guy. Lots of people thought it was a rebound thing. Maybe it was, but I don't think so because I had chances to go out with other people and didn't.

All my girlfriends knew how unhappy I was about Marvin, and they saw how happy I'd gotten with the football player. So they thought I should continue seeing the football player until his wife came to town; why not, they said, cling to it a little longer. My girlfriends figure you should enjoy life now because you might not be here tomorrow to enjoy it. So I kept seeing him about six more months, sometimes even when his wife was in town. Behind her back.

He said he wished he knew me when he was single; he wished that I was the mother of his two children. And I wished it were me, too. Once out of the clear blue sky he told me he couldn't divorce his wife, that she'd go crazy without him, wouldn't know what to do without him. And it was a sort of shock to me because I'd never said anything to him about getting a divorce.

I told him that I never expected him to leave his wife for me. I said, "We can't be happy on somebody else's sorrow. We just can't do that." You know, if someone divorces someone and then meets someone, that's different than divorcing someone for someone else.

O

As men, football players are more manly and more intelligent than baseball players. A lot of baseball players carry on really dull conversations, and of course both kinds are all egotistical. If baseball players didn't have the game going for them, they'd probably be a milk truck driver because most sign team contracts straight out of high school. But football players have more going for them—college educations. And they give great parties.

There was this one for a whole pro football team that was called a stag, but most of the players brought babes. The wives weren't supposed to know. The party was at a player's house, and they served crab cioppino, garlic bread and a funny kind of drink: Gatorade mixed with vodka. Everyone was having a good time, and all of a sudden this one player who is usually very quiet and reserved jumps off a balcony and drops his drawers. A couple of cop cars are parked in a drive-in restaurant across the street. But they didn't bother the party.

Upstairs in one of the bedrooms an older woman, in her late thirties or early forties, was taking care of different guys that wanted taking care of. I saw her peek her head out the door once to see who was next. The player's weren't lined up, just that one would come out and another would go in. The woman was just a fan, I guess. She liked being around football players. But I don't think the players thought too highly of her. They were nice to her though, you know. I kind of felt sorry for her, because I thought she must have a problem, that she had to do something like that—oral copulation, you know—to feel like one of the group, one of the girls.

()

If I had known years ago what I know now, I never would have left Marvin. I never even would have told him I hired the private detective. Now I realize that all men cheat. I don't care what walk of life they're in or what their line of work is. They all go out. Which was really disheartening to me; I couldn't believe it. Athletes do it more because they're away from their wives more and can set up permanent girlfriends in each town that their wife won't find out about. These girls will wait for them.

It was hard for me to adjust as an individual after the divorce. You know, out in public I was looked upon just as Marvin's ex-wife, not Rachel. And people would talk about me, whatever I did. I wasn't even doing anything, and people would say I was. It would upset me and I'd call up my dad and mother and tell them things that had come back to me. I went through periods where I would stay home most of the time because I couldn't hack the gossip.

Like, I went to this one bar where most of the athletes went after games. And if I knew someone on the team that was in town I would naturally say hi and talk to them. And sometimes I'd give them a ride back to their hotel after the bar closed, maybe have coffee or breakfast with them. It was automatically assumed by people that—no matter who I left the bar with—that person was supposed to be laying me.

Sometimes some of Marvin's old baseball friends, even a couple of his teammates, would try to put the make on me if I ran into them. I mean, I thought they were sick. Sick. There's something wrong with guys like that. They're supposed to be your friend—and here they are trying to get me in bed. That even happened before the divorce was official. It upset me. Sometimes I would cry. I wondered if it was me, if it was something I'd said that made them try. Or, if it was really just them. I didn't understand it at all.

It took me a couple of years to feel completely free. Maybe because I'm such a wild dresser now I come across as something I'm not. But that doesn't bother me anymore. I keep myself pretty well in hand and under control, because, well, if I don't ever let myself care for a man the way I cared for Marvin, I won't ever get hurt like he hurt me. Because he crushed me. He just tore everything down that I ever was. I had to rebuild myself. I just thought I was a big nothing and that was why he went out on me. The first time he told me I was pretty was when he broke up the marriage. But then he said, "Beauty isn't everything."

I mean, I went through four years of marriage trying to please and being told that whatever I did wasn't good enough. I'll never let anybody do that to me again. If a guy starts closing in, I'll just turn around and run.

a wife

sandy bando... *thirty-year-old former nurse, graduate of Villanova, daughter of a New Jersey obstetrician-gynecologist. Long, dark hair and dancing, dark eyes. Married in early 1969 to Oakland Athletics' third baseman-captain Sal Bando, who twinkles at times himself. Both are Catholic, but Sandy less rigid and less of an Italian stereotype. They have two small boys. Sal met Sandy at a night club in Puerto Rico; they wooed cross-country for more than a year. Their rambling ranch-style home sits at the end of a short, cul-de-sac street in the Oakland suburb of Danville, California. Sandy speaks openly, quickly, warmly. She is not necessarily representative of a professional athlete's wife; merely one of them. And very pretty, too.*

I will honestly say that before Sal and I got married, my father talked to me about the problems of being the wife of a professional athlete. He respects Sal tremendously, and they have a fantastic rapport. But at that time my father said to me, "I just want to tell you what kind of life you're getting into. For one thing, Sandy, you're not used to being alone."

Which I wasn't. Even when I was in college, I had a roommate.

My dad went on and on about my being out on the West Coast with a husband who was going to do a lot of traveling if he managed to stay in the big leagues. My dad said, "There are certain things you're going to learn you have to live with. Don't be blinded by the fact you just say you love him."

I said, "I know what I'm getting into."

And I didn't. That's the funny thing. I really didn't.

()

The first year we were married I was paranoid about what might be going on with Sal on the road. Definitely paranoid. I called him in Chicago once at two o'clock in the morning, their time. There was no answer, yet I was led to believe he had a midnight curfew. I found out later nothing really had happened, but I kept imagining things simply because of everything that was revolving around us on the team that year.

It seemed as though there was a lot of, you know, smutty kind of business. And the wife of this one infielder—he's no longer with the A's—kept saying that she could ruin every marriage on our club because she knew something in the past or present of the players that could, you know, cause problems. So naturally I started assuming that, well, Sal isn't really any different.

I didn't really know what he was like because most of our fifteen-month courtship was by mail. I mean, all I thought was that I just really loved him. I felt he was a great person, that he came from a nice family background in the sense his morals were good, and what have you. He seemed to be a very reliable, responsible person, and this is what impressed me. Besides being passionately infatuated with him. But I really didn't know what his feelings were on other women. I had to develop this kind of security with him *after* we were married.

I confronted him in our newlywed days with these things I'd heard from other wives. I kept on badgering him. I almost accused him of seeing another woman, because I'd heard that other players were doing it. And to this day, *I don't really know.*

Now I have so much faith in him that I trust him. But in those early days, when I would talk to him about someone else's problems, he would say to me, "Well, just don't worry about it because it's not you." That's all he would give me, though. That, and then he'd say, "Trust me." I felt I needed a more demonstrative display of a way which I could trust

209   *sandy bando*

him. But there was no way he could do it. Somehow now, though, he has gained my complete respect, and complete trust.

Yet I know that Sal is aware of another beautiful woman. Definitely. An attractive girl can turn his head, and naturally so. But I just truly believe that I've worked hard enough pleasing him myself. I mean, I feel that if a man is going to leave his wife for any reason—just for an affair here or there—well then somehow the woman in his life is failing him.

He didn't trust women when we were first married. Okay, he was hitting me with the same thing I was throwing at him. I asked him what he meant, and he said that when he was in the minor leagues he actually saw women that were cheating on their husbands when the fellas went on road trips. He had this opinion that women are no good. I felt then that he treated me like I was a woman of no worth and I resented this because I just didn't feel that way.

At first he dictated everything I was to do: what time I had to be in, who I could talk to, who I could associate with. He didn't like some of the girls on the club that I associated with because of their backgrounds. One of the wives on the club then apparently dated a lot of fellas on another major league team and had a bad reputation. I got friendly with her, and Sal didn't like me spending time with her. He said, "Fellas will see you and think that you're like her."

I said, "Well, that's your opinion. It's not bothering me."

0

I forced Sal one time to tell me about what the guys did on the road. You know how? And this shows how catty I was. I made up stories. "I heard, hon, that so and so did this. Is it true?"

He'd say, "You didn't really hear that, honey," I'd say that yes, I did.

Finally he said to me, "Look, hon, what goes on stays in the clubhouse. We have an unwritten law that none of us talks about each other. I'm sorry. I can't tell you anything."

And Sal has not. But I know that other players tell because I hear it from wives. The wives are the ones that reveal everything, and they don't even do it consciously at times. It just comes out.

A lot of wives try to block these things out of their minds, and I think they do that because they are insecure. They don't want to lose. You know, to a lot of girls being married is a sense of security, especially when you have children. An awful lot of the wives can't picture themselves without this man.

I think the first thing I would do if I found out Sal was having an affair on the road would be just to run away. I couldn't...I wouldn't...I'd have to go away. I couldn't face him. I know what would happen, too. He'd come home, and like all the other arguments we've had, no matter what about, he'd tell me that he loves me and this is what I'd need at the time to hear. I'd submit and fall and believe and accept all the apologies. But two weeks later I'd be looking at him and thinking about it and hating him, and then all of a sudden this thing would come out and I would start destroying us.

I know there are some wives who are aware of their husbands having affairs, and they've accepted the situation. One wife like this loves her husband to this day. She says, "You know, we had a problem but we're working it out. I understand it." Maybe she *can* accept it.

Then there's another wife who had a notion about her husband having an affair but just didn't want to think about it. It was a year ago that she had an inkling. She thought: *maybe*. Consequently she went out and did stupid things herself. I can't say that she was ignorant, because I really can't believe someone could be *that* ignorant, but she was dumb like her husband. She started having too platonic a relationship with another man. The player would come over to this other man and say, "Is my wife here?"

And the other fella would say, "She's not here now. Leave."

You can't tell me that that player didn't have enough intelligence to say, "What's my wife doing here with you, anyway?" He didn't know if she'd been there earlier. All he knew was that she wasn't there with this fella *now*.

Sal once said to me that most athletes' wives are pretty good-looking. But to be honest, all the wives I've met are just everything that normal girls are. It's just a bad generalization that all athletes' wives are pretty girls from school—cheerleader types. And the funny thing is, not all the ballplayers are like the so-called Adonises that we think they are.

I guess that most athletes label women. Like: she's just a broad, she's a ballpark girl. Or: she's just a wife, a domestic. The athletes can get away from this domestic life. In a way, their existence is a very glamorous one. People are always after them, wanting their autographs, treating them as celebrities. The players are in and out of hotels, always being recognized. And here's the little old girl, left at home to take care of things that a man would be doing maybe if *he* was home. But no, you're left at home. You're expected to run the house, run your business affairs, raise the kids.

Just the other day Linda (Mrs. Gene) Tenace told me, "Gene expects me to sit home and just stay with the kids all the time. He was mad at me for going to a party with the neighbors. He doesn't expect me to have any kind of social life. He doesn't want me to enjoy anything without him."

And I said, "Well, Linda, maybe he just feels that your whole life has to be only him."

But don't you see? It really can't be; he's away a lot.

()

Spring training of 1970 was the first time I ever saw any of the things that I had heard all those rumors about. It was an innocent thing this one night at The Sands in Phoenix, where most of the club was staying.

Sal and I were coming back from dinner and walked past one of the players' rooms. There were a lot of familiar faces in there drinking, and there was a bunch of girls in the room with them.

As I went by the open door, one player came out and seemed almost apologetic that I should have seen him. The door was wide open, so they weren't really trying to hide anything. But still they didn't want me to see, because I knew very well that this one player's wife wasn't in Phoenix.

The player asked Sal if he wanted to come in and have a drink. And I said, "If you want to go in, go ahead. I'll go up to our room." He didn't, but what I saw in that party room jibed with some of the rumors I'd heard about a few of the wives having problems.

Then when the season opened, more substantial information started coming in. And all of a sudden it seemed like there was this mad dash by the wives to go on a road trip. A lot of the girls wanted to go along to Anaheim. Yes, Anaheim was the big one. I don't know if it was because that's so close to Oakland and was cheaper to get to or because that's where all the rumors were coming from.

But I do remember that one wife told me a rumor that such and such a player was picked up in Anaheim by a girl driving a Volkswagen. So immediately I hit Sal with it.

He said, "That shows you what a stupid so-and-so that wife is. The girl happened to be the player's cousin."

The response was always something that made the person who started the rumor look like a real fool. A very surprised fool.

()

Once when I was visiting Sal at his apartment in Oakland at the time we were dating, I found a whole bunch of

213 *sandy bando*

telephone numbers in his wallet. He was out of the apartment, and I went through his dresser drawers looking for letters and that sort of thing. Terrible. But I really can say I don't do that anymore. I did it then because I was dating him. I'm not going to look for it, you know. Let's just say that I was younger then. (Laughs quietly.) It's a question of maturity.

When I asked Sal then about the phone numbers I'd found, he told me they belonged to a married pitcher. I think the fella is still kicking around in the majors someplace. So you know what I did—fat mouth me? I go over to two wives on the club and tell them about it. These were two girls who were trying to help me get Sal to marry me. I told them not to tell anybody about this pitcher's phone numbers. I truly believed they wouldn't open their mouths. Well, they did. They told their husbands and a couple of other people, and the word got back to the pitcher.

He goes up to Sal and says, "Tell your girlfriend to keep her mouth shut. I'm happily married, I've got a couple of kids. So tell your girlfriend to keep quiet."

Sal then comes to me and says, "You go and tell those wives that the phone numbers were mine. Say that I told you they were the pitcher's because I didn't want you to get mad at me."

And that's what I did. It seemed to me the only logical thing to do because we weren't married and it couldn't hurt me. But it could hurt the pitcher's wife. That was my introduction into keeping my mouth shut.

The funny part is that to this day the pitcher still has a thing about conquering girls.

()

Maybe I'm putting too much trust in men, but anytime there is something going on I can't help but feel that a woman has instigated it. On the whole, women are an

unbelievable group of people. We really *are*. We play games.
We connive. We can make men believe things that aren't
really true. We can manipulate them. I consider myself a
straight-laced girl, but I played the game to get Sal. Just like
every other woman.

Recently we were at some little place, a restaurant with a
neat little bar and small combo. When we walked in, Sal said,
"This is the kind of place I go to, honey, for a drink after a
game."

I said, "That's nice." And I do a double-take at him.
What's immediately going through my mind is: there's got to
be a waitress at that kind of place, or maybe just a couple of
girls who'll walk in and sit down waiting to be noticed by the
players. Sal and all the men in the world aren't going to tell
me they wouldn't look at these girls. But the thing is, a girl
gives the come-on sign.

Let's face it: there are some women who are simply
celebrity seekers; then there are others who are sex-
oriented—looking, you know, for an affair by night. There
also are some that are really down-to-earth, basic, nice girls
who just want to meet a fella. Look at myself, for instance. I
met Sal at a night club but I didn't go there with the
intention of meeting him. I went to the club because I
wanted to see the entertainers. I didn't know there would be
athletes there.

And the athletes are susceptible. They can always say that
a woman approached them. Sal told me one time, "The guys
got this player drunk and sent a girl up to his room. What
could he do? He was stone drunk."

That I just couldn't accept—the fact the fellas on the club
thought it was a big joke to get this guy drunk and send a girl
up to his room for an affair. "He was so drunk, he wasn't
responsible for his actions," Sal said.

And I said, "How can you say a person is not responsible
for their actions? If you're responsible in the first place, you'll
always keep that much sense about youself." I just wonder
when some of these players are going to get off their celebrity

merry-go-round. I'm demanding a mature response from these guys.

Sal thought what happened to the player was understandable but he didn't think it was funny. He said, "I would never do it."

I told him it *could* happen to him. I said, "You trying to tell me that someday you might get stone drunk and go through with that kind of thing and then say you didn't know what you were doing? I'm supposed to accept that? Maybe what you really mean is that you won't get so totally drunk because you know I wouldn't take you back."

The times we were in Arizona, Sal refused to take me to any of the places the players went at night. He told me he was just protecting me. He said, "I don't want you to see anything you wouldn't understand."

I guess he pictures me living in a little, innocent glass cage, that I don't see or hear anything evil. But he has to realize that I've grown up. I was naive when I met him. But by now I think I know what goes on.

I once kidded him about me going down to this place in Anaheim, this bar where I hear players go after a game. He said, "You're not going to do that."

I said, "Yes. Sometimes I would just like to lurk in a corner of the bar and watch all of you and how you act."

You want to know something? I want to do it but yet I don't. I don't want to be disappointed by anybody.